Teacher-to-Teacher Series

TEACHING TECHNOLOGY with

NEA Teacher-to-Teacher Books

Printing History

First Printing: July 1999

NOTE: The opinions expressed in this book should not be construed as representing the policy or position of the National Education Association. Materials published by the NEA Professional Library are intended to be discussion documents for educators who are concerned with specialized interests of the profession.

CREDITS: *Series Editor:* Sabrina Holcomb. *Cover and Book Design:* Linda Brunson. *Series Design:* NoBul Graphics.

This book is printed on acid free paper.

 This book is printed with soy ink.

ACID FREE
∞

Teaching with technology.
    p. cm.— (Teacher to teacher series)
"NEA teacher-to-teacher books."
ISBN 0-8106-2912-7
1. Teaching—United States—Aids and devices. 2. Computer-assisted instruction—United States. 3. Educational technology—United States. I. National Education Association of the United States. II. Series.

LB1044.88.T44 1999
371.33—dc21   99-33085
                                                                                    CIP

Contents

How To Use this Book

Teaching with Technology is no ordinary book. It is one of NEA's Teacher-to-Teacher Books, in which classroom and resource teachers speak directly to other teachers—like you—about their efforts to improve the quality of teaching and learning.

Printed in the upper right-hand corner of every book in the series is a routing slip that encourages you to pass the book on to colleagues once you've read it— in other words, to spread the word about school change.

Previous topics in the series covered areas such as large-scale school change, student assessment, multi-age grouping, integrated thematic teaching, parent involvement, inclusion, innovative discipline, multiple intelligences, technology for diverse learners, how to get grants and free resources, and peer mentoring.

Read the Six Stories

Inside this book you will find stories from six or more teachers across the country. Each story illustrates step-by-step how they integrate technology into their school curriculum. They describe what worked and didn't work in the process. Each chapter includes diagrams, checklists, or tables you can use in your efforts to develop, facilitate, or improve similar programs in your district.

Reader Reflections

At the end of each chapter, you can jot down your immediate thoughts and ideas to follow up on in our reader reflections page.

You see, the purpose of Teacher-to-Teacher Books is not only to spread the word about school change but to encourage other teachers to participate in its exploration.

Discuss Your Thoughts with Others

Once you've routed a book through your school, you can meet with colleagues who contributed to the Reader Reflections sections and expand upon your thoughts.

Go Online

The communication and sharing does not have to stop there. Visit the NEA home page on the World Wide Web, your gateway to resources and information that can help you improve teaching and learning in your school. You can find us at http://www.nea.org. From there, the Professional Library Web site is just a click away.

Introduction

When students come to me with long lists of Web links they've discovered on a particular topic, I can stop them in their tracks with four words: What does it mean?

Middle school teacher Ferdi Serim voices a dilemma facing many of today's teachers. In a world where schools are connected to the Web and students surf the Net with ease, teachers are discovering that it's not enough for kids to be computer literate. They need to be information literate as well.

A decade ago, when schools around the country first started using computers, many teachers weren't sure how to make the best use of them. Initially, the emphasis was on creating a computer curriculum in which students—and teachers—cycled through the lab to learn about technology. Now learning has evolved to the next stage, and teachers face the challenge of using technology to transform the curriculum and revamp instruction.

What does this mean for students? And how are schools meeting this challenge? Naturally, not all schools are on the same level; they fall at different points on the technology continuum. But the most successful schools have a common denominator—they balance computer literacy with curricular integration to create a strong, well-rounded program for their students.

Students come to school with markedly different levels of technology skills, and schools are responsible for making sure all their students have the basic skills they need to function in a world that's increasingly technology-dependent. In addition, technology demands have grown so complex that schools often need a resource specialist to troubleshoot the technology and a curricular specialist to integrate the technology into core subject areas.

This book describes the personal odysseys of six teachers who have used technology to transform their teaching. They share the strategies they've used to start up programs, get around stumbling blocks, and find needed funds for equipment and software. They also describe how they use technology to help their students develop the critical thinking and interpersonal skills they need to become better learners.

- Ferdi Serim, a computer resource teacher in the Princeton Regional Schools, works with social studies, science, and language arts classes on a Year 2000 project that explores the impact of society's reliance on technology. He also lists specific technological tools teachers can use to help students develop higher-order thinking skills in any subject area.

• Roosevelt-Perry Elementary, a Title I school, is a State Model Technology School that uses technology in wonderfully creative ways to enhance every-day learning. Technology coordinator Janis Lowe describes how she and her colleagues use technology to improve reading, help teachers control their workload, and link the school to the surrounding community.

• Al Bode, a high school Spanish teacher, uses the Internet to provide his students with a cultural and linguistic immersion that would otherwise be hard to come by in rural Iowa. Bode gives an overview of his Web site, which contains unique materials created for student use and over 110 major links to resources for teachers and students of foreign language.

• Library/Media Specialist Elaine Snider has evolved from teaching library skills with a card catalog to helping students prepare multimedia reports with sophisticated software. She describes how she works with classroom teachers and gives a valuable grade-by-grade account of elementary students' technology projects and corresponding curricular skills.

• English teacher Beth Cristensen was once terrified of computers. Now she and her eighth grade class have an award-winning Web site with an international audience. Cristensen describes the multimedia projects she uses to give traditional English lessons a new-tech twist.

• When students complete Stephen Lalonde's class on radio and video production, they're ready for the real world of work. In fact, some of his students run a production company that does professional jobs for real clients. Lolonde gives teachers a detailed blueprint for starting an RTV class in their school.

Whether you're a novice or a technology maven, we hope the stories in *Teaching with Technology* provide inspiration for your classroom and useful information for your school's technology program.

—Sabrina Holcomb
Series Editor

HOPE OR HYPE?

This teacher found that the real challenge isn't in how to use "wires and boxes" but in how students use computer technology to think.

1 Computers—hope or hype? A few years ago, when NEA and The Learning Channel's School Stories did a segment with that title, they interviewed a number of people in our school district, including me. We explained how we integrate technology into the curriculum by demonstrating a few projects we were working on at the time. The interviewers asked a lot of tough questions around one main theme—do computers in the school bring hope for our educational system, or is it all a lot of hype?

The answer may surprise you. In my opinion, everything depends on the teaching. Good teaching is strengthened by technology, but only with a lot of work. Weak teaching does not benefit. My experience as a computer resource teacher in two New Jersey school districts has

FERDI SERIM
Princeton Regional Schools
Princeton, New Jersey

led me to conclude that 85 percent of the learning happens away from the computer, in terms of the conversations that become possible because of what has come across the screen.

The Real Princeton

Because Princeton University's Ivy League status is so well-known, many people assume that students in the Princeton Regional Schools (PRS) district are all walking around with silver spoons in their mouths. This is not the case. PRS is a diverse district of more than 3,000 students, 30 percent of whom are minority. We do have students whose parents are Nobel Prize winners and

Eighty-five percent of the learning happens away from the computer.

MacArthur Foundation "genius grant" recipients. In recent years, we have also had a growing number of children who moved to Princeton from Central America and are attending school for the first time in their lives.

The district has one high, one middle, and four elementary schools. I came to John Witherspoon (JW) Middle School five years ago to help guide the use of technology for learning. At the time, I was the only computer teacher in the district. The district has since hired two additional computer resource teachers who cover the elementary schools and one more at the middle school.

I came from the nearby West Windsor/Plainsboro schools. There, a single phone line and modem transformed my computer lab into a launchpad for activities that had my students designing and piloting solar sailers to the moon, corresponding with Russian students, and receiving media attention in *Scientific American* and the *Los Angeles Times* and on National Public Radio. When Princeton Regional Schools recruited me to guide their use of technology for learning, I already had tenure and "a successful practice." What could entice me to leave "Shangri-La"? The chance to jump five years into the future!

Do You Have a Wizard?

Whenever I do workshops at other districts or at conferences, I ask people: "Who's your wizard?" Technology demands have grown so much in complexity, one person cannot expect to have all the qualifications to handle both the curriculum and the technical aspects. Just figuring out which networking software to use has become a full-time job!

Everyone needs a wizard, and in our case it's Peter Thompson. Thanks to the work of Peter, our District Technical Coordinator, and Ira Fuchs, Princeton University's Director of Computing, Princeton Regional Schools enjoy a level of connectivity that is ahead of most of the rest of the world. Peter and Ira found a way to use cable TV to connect all six of our schools into a wide area network. They then wired each computer in every lab and classroom to the Internet through the university, so we can connect at speeds from 100 to 300 times faster than a modem.

Besides a wizard in charge of "wires and boxes," a school

needs someone to take educational leadership of the technology. This is the role that I was asked to take in Princeton: to discover how to advance learning in an environment where questions about speed or number of connected computers have simply disappeared.

What I've found is that when you take the focus away from troubleshooting the technical aspects—worrying about the wires and boxes—you can then concentrate on having the vision and skill to integrate the technology into the curriculum.

Integrated or Stand-Alone?

When I began work in Princeton, I felt that our activities should support achievement of existing curricular goals through the appropriate application of technology, and not add technology as another set of curricular goals. Instead of a "computer literacy curriculum," in which students would cycle through the lab to "learn about technology," we focused on "curricular integration." In this way, the lab became a resource tailored to the instructional objectives of every teacher who entered.

Team Teaching

I have been team teaching for every period of the last five years. There isn't a subject I haven't helped some teacher in our middle school teach, from the traditional "core subjects" (science, math, language arts, social studies) to art, French, Spanish, health, and music—because there isn't a subject that doesn't depend on the skills of thinking.

Applications Lab

My lab is called the Applications Lab because students come to apply technology tools to their everyday learning. The lab has 26 MAC LC 575 computers, networked via Ethernet, running on AppleShare, and sharing LaserWriter and DeskWriter printers. These are the same computers that I opened the lab with five years ago. Although they connect to the Internet rapidly, they crash about once a class period when they download large graphics or access complex applications. I've also lost four chairs this year when students rocked back and forth

Besides a wizard in charge of "wires and boxes," a school needs someone to take educational leadership of the technology.

so hard as they worked that the chairs literally broke!

In 1997-1998, a second computer lab opened at JW, staffed by another teacher, where students take a course to learn word processing, keyboarding, presentation software, etc. It's called the Skills Lab. We found that we needed to introduce computer skills, particularly to sixth graders, when it became clear that they came to middle school with very different levels of comfort and background with computer operations.

Setting up a course like this may seem to counter my philosophical thrust, but actually it proves my point. Too often we hear discussions that generate more heat than light, about

Too often discussions about computer labs versus classroom computers generate more heat than light.

whether there should be computer labs or classroom computers, or whether technology should be integrated within the curriculum or taught as a specific skill set. The answer is both! When I came to JW as the only computer teacher, I decided to focus on integration. As the program grew, we realized that the challenge of equity demanded that we level the playing field for students who don't have computers at home. That's when we added "fundamentals" to our program. Without the basic skills, the higher order thinking skills I use to challenge students couldn't work for all children.

Teaching Students to THINK

An inquiry-based curriculum introduces the higher order skills of gathering, evaluating, analyzing, and presenting. Technological tools exist for each of these skills. Both students and teachers need to be aware of the choices they have so that they effectively use the right tool for the job at hand.

We're used to seeing computer programs referred to by their function (for example, word processor or spreadsheet). They are less often grouped in the context of the four higher order thinking skills. Taken this way, tools can be blended to meet specific purposes.

Gathering

Once we have identified a topic to study, we gather the words, images, or visualizations that cover as much information from as many perspectives as possible. Classroom research today takes the text-based references familiar to most adults and augments them with CD-ROMs containing music, speeches, diagrams, animations, and film clips. Likewise, the Internet makes original data from universities and government research databases accessible to teachers and their students. In fact, there's so much information available, students need to learn how to search efficiently and effectively. For example, our students are now doing a project on the implications of the Year 2000. They began by giving their opinion about what they thought might happen on January 1, 2000, and then gathered information on the Internet to support or refute their conclusions.

Specific tools that support gathering skills include word processors, CD-ROM references, Internet search engines (Lycos, AltaVista, and Yahoo are popular choices), and older tools such as gopher, archie, veronica, FTP, plus a host of E-mail and newsgroup destinations.

Evaluating

Separating the info-gems from info-glut is both an individual and a group activity. Students need to know what questions to ask and whom to ask in order to advance their knowledge on a topic. In the Year 2K project, students gathered information and then, as a group, they evaluated the validity of the information and the sources they found. They concluded, for example, that information about potential Y2K disasters on a Web site of a company that sells Y2K-related products might not be objective.

Specific tools that support evaluating include group conferencing and E-mail software, as well as numerous newsgroups and "listservs" organized around any imaginable topic. Stand-alone applications that don't require network access include word processors and graphics programs.

Analyzing

This is one area in which the computer provides capabilities unimagined by previous generations. Spreadsheets, databases, and graphing programs have transformed analysis of numerical data, allowing patterns to emerge from massive collections

Students need to know what questions to ask in order to separate the info gems from the info glut.

of information—provided we know which questions to ask. In the Y2K project, students had to analyze the implications of the material they found—for example, determining that maybe the Y2K problem has different implications in the United States than in other countries.

Recently, image-processing software has appeared on student desktops, previously available only to mainframe researchers at places like the Jet Propulsion Laboratory or National Institutes of Health. This software (such as NIH Image and RasMol) makes it possible to visualize relationships and trends in ways that couldn't be done otherwise. Fortunately for

Fortunately for school districts, much of the best software is available for free on the Internet.

school districts, much of the best software is available for free on the Internet, thanks to funding from the National Science Foundation, NASA, and other organizations. A host of spreadsheets, database, and graphing applications (including integrated packages such as ClarisWorks and Microsoft Works) are also good tools for students to use in analyzing.

Presenting

Publishing used to mean books, magazines, or newspapers from printing presses. Today students are publishing their own findings using videotape, multimedia computer programs, and information servers on the Internet. They can access each other's work using sophisticated information robots, which burrow through global networks to retrieve documents based on keyword searches. Of course, students are also using powerful desktop publishing programs with nearly the same capabilities professional publishers enjoy. Our students are publishing their Y2K findings on our school Web site and will be preparing presentations for local officials and media.

Specific tools include desktop publishing applications such as PageMaker or Quark Express; hypermedia authoring or multimedia programs such as HyperStudio, Linkway, and HyperCard; and many full-featured word processors such as WordPerfect and Microsoft Word.

Information Literacy

Most adults grew up going to the library reference section to do research. Students today can access network and other computer-based information in forms that go beyond traditional text. Locating and using these resources effectively is a discipline unto itself. Students will need these skills for their future success. That's why familiarity with these resources, as well as the purposes that each resource most effectively serves, is a vital early experience.

This particular set of skills is known as Information Literacy. The American Association of School Librarians has established suggested competencies every person needs to become a lifelong learner, and, personally,

I'm encouraged by this development. In a world where every computer a student encounters is connected to the Internet, I've been dismayed by how many students have yet to develop the reading, thinking, and communicating skills to effectively make use of the opportunities such a connection provides. When students come to me with long lists of Web links they have discovered on a particular topic, I can stop them in their tracks with four words: What does it mean?

Students who are information literate should be able to access, evaluate, and use information alone and in groups—for their own knowledge and for the good of the community.

I'd like to share an experience with you that shows how all this comes together. Ironically, it's a project about the new millennium. And although we have done some exciting things in this project, it also reminds me that

technology is not the be-all solution to ensuring that our students are literate for the 21st century.

Year 2K and You!

There are plentiful and conflicting messages in the media and on the Internet about what might happen to computers all over the world as December 31, 1999, rolls over to January 1, 2000. This seemed to be a great opportunity to introduce students to systems thinking and the role of technology in an interdependent world. During the 1998-1999 school year, I've been working with teachers and students in all three grades of our school on a project called Year 2K and You.

Our purpose has been to provide students with an authentic, challenging task that allows them to discover the interdependent systems responsible for providing our quality of life. They have discovered that these

systems are comprised of people, and that the performance or disruptions that happen in one system can have unanticipated influences on other systems. Finally, they are learning which organizations, institutions, and individuals work in the systems of the Princeton community, informing these people and organizations of the results of their research; investigating what preparations have been made; and reporting their findings to our community.

Reinforcing Skills

Each September, I must "introduce" students to the applications lab and help them set up their E-mail accounts and electronic workspaces (an area on our network fileserver for each student, accessible only by his or her password). This year, I devised the Y2K project as the vehicle for introducing network operations, Internet searching,

ED's Oasis Treasure Zone

Our project design benefited from two resources found in the ED's Oasis "Treasure Zone." ED's Oasis (http://www.edsoasis.org), if you don't already know it, is a great Web site for teachers because its staff of educators and editors sifts through and evaluates the thousands of instructional resource sites out there. ED's then provides links or describes those that are high quality, curriculum aligned, standards supporting, and student centered. We found links to two sites that particularly helped us:
the Big Six Information Management Skills (http://www.big6.com) and
Nueva Library Research Goals
(http://www.nueva.pvt.k12.ca.us/~debbie/library/research/research.html).

and collaboration in a networked environment. For this project, students also needed to know how to use a Web browser and copy and paste between applications (word processing, multimedia authoring, etc.) that are running concurrently. We conducted our introduction to the Y2K project in such a way as to reinforce these skills and provide peer coaching for new students or others who may not yet have developed these skills.

Project Design

How can a glitch in a computer cause all this fuss? Thinking about what might happen on January 1, 2000, leads to a deeper understanding of the interconnected world we live in, and how different it is from the world in which our parents and grandparents grew up. Sure, you could do without your computer—but how about money? Or electricity? Or food? This led us to design a project in which students had to decide the importance of this phenomenon for themselves and then find out what our community is doing to prepare for the Year 2K.

The result was a five-phase plan for the 1998-1999 school year. Besides reading about it here, you can see the work of our students on the John Witherspoon Web site (http://www.prs.k12.nj.us/Schools/JohnWitherspoon/) or read a synopsis of the project on the ED's Oasis site.

In fall 1998, the project received first prize in ED's MasterSearch contest for the best lesson plan in grades 7 through 9 that makes effective use of the Internet.

Phase 1: Building a Foundation of Knowledge

In the first phase, students conducted research to learn more about the topic. My role as teacher was to organize the materials and facilitate the process. The social studies, science, and language arts teachers and I developed activities for each grade that connected with core curriculum goals. For example, eighth graders study civics, so they studied the governmental structure of our community to identify the individuals and organizations they would interview to learn about Y2K preparations. Seventh graders study world cultures, so they compared and contrasted U.S. needs for power, heat, food, and security with the needs of other civilizations around the world, and they examined the potential impact of Y2K on these societies. Sixth graders study ancient civilizations, so they compared and contrasted how we solve our needs today with how prior civilizations solved them.

During this first phase, students worked in the computer lab over a period of two weeks and then followed up with discussions in their classrooms, led by social studies, science, and language arts teachers, as it became appropriate to meeting their curricular objectives.

Phase 2: Sharing the Knowledge

In the second phase, students used E-mail and our conferencing system to share what they learned and to develop a contingency plan for their families. My role as a teacher was to "set up" the discussion, by challenging students to trace the source of

common societal needs. For example, I asked, "What will you eat for lunch today?" For each item, I asked, "Where was it this morning? Last week? The week before that? The month before that?" Soon the distribution system for our food supply came into focus. We had a similar discussion about energy and examined the systems that provide communications and other critical services. For example, the students first said that each Princeton resident should withdraw $1,000 from the bank in late 1999 to have on hand and then learned that the banks would not have enough cash in their reserves if this were to happen!

Following a discussion, students used the school's Web site (http://www.prs.k12.nj.us/Schools/JohnWitherspoon/Year2K/y2k.htm) to examine evidence for their opinions and to develop questions to ask community

leaders about the extent of Princeton's preparations.

Initially, students E-mailed their work to me, and I reviewed and analyzed it. However, they quickly realized that, with this method, only I could see what everyone thought. In order to "share our brains," we needed a different method. So in the next activity, the students used the electronic conferencing system (FirstClass Intranet Server, which allows us to use bulletin board systems and chat systems to support collaboration) to post

Students posted their votes about whether they consider Y2K problems to be "for real" or "a hoax."

their vote about whether they consider Y2K problems to be "for real" or "a hoax." They then discussed and critiqued their votes on-line.

Phase 3: Investigations in the Community

As I write this, we are working on the next phases of the project. In the third phase, teams of students will synthesize questions and prepare to interview the appropriate experts and leaders in our community to determine the anticipated impact of Y2K in Princeton and what people should be doing now to prepare. The Nueva Library Advice for Research on a Complex Topic

The Y2K lesson is effective because it uses technology to explore the societal impact of reliance upon technology.

(http://www.nueva.pvt.k12.ca.us /~debbie/library/research/advice.html) will be very helpful to our students at this stage. Not all 735 students will go out to interview, but we will set it up so that the questions of all students will get asked by a smaller group, and the results will be made available to everyone. This investigative phase will also engage the considerable number of our school's parents who work professionally on Y2K issues, as well as other computer professionals who work at local universities and research organizations.

Phase 4: Synthesizing the Findings

In the fourth phase, students will synthesize their findings, using a range of technologies from word processing to multimedia authoring. Examples will be posted on our Web site throughout the year. Student teams will evaluate the contributions of other students to ensure high-quality products.

Phase 5: Presenting the Findings to the Community

In the fifth phase, students will make community presentations—to the Board of Education, through the PTO newsletter, via cable TV, and through reports to local newspapers. They will also make "press conference" style presentations to interested community groups. Our students expect that they will be among the most knowledgeable people on Y2K in our community at this point in the project— and they're probably right!

Assessment

We're using our Intranet to gather student performance data over the life of the project. For instance, we can monitor traffic on E-mail and in the conferences to see how many students post messages. Our computer lab is open before and after school, and we can see how many students do independent work during these times. Representative messages and summary screens will be made available on our Web site as the project progresses. The site itself documents the evolution of the project as groups report their findings and additional resources become available. Additionally, students will "peer review" submissions by other students, as will parent and community experts.

I also hope to use an assessment matrix that I prepared several years ago to observe whether students have mastered the skills and standards that link to the Information Literacy Standards (see reproducible). I spent one of the hardest weeks of my professional life figuring out the specific, observable behaviors that indicate mastery of each of the standards!

What It All Means

I think the Y2K lesson is particularly effective because it uses technology to explore the societal impact of reliance upon technology. It exposes students to compelling arguments from both "pro" and "con" viewpoints and requires students to move into the higher order thinking skills where technology can have its best results. Our research moves beyond being an academic exercise when we go into our own community and begin to explore the systems that support "life as we know it" and the interdependencies that are required to sustain these systems.

So, hope or hype? This is our challenge in teaching with technology: to develop information literacy in all our students and to help them use technology as a tool for higher order thinking. No matter how much the technology advances, it still all boils down to good teaching!

Gaining Skill in Using Technology as a Tool for Interpersonal Learning

Objectives	Measurable Goals *
Technology Application	Students will learn how to use various forms of technology to improve their performance.
Cooperative Learning	Students will learn how to operate in groups, and their achievement and attitudes will reflect the skills learned.
Language Arts	Students will acquire a positive attitude toward reading, read with better comprehension, and write more creatively and analytically.

Getting Results: the Relationship of Measurable Goals to Information Literacy Standards **

Information Literacy **	Technology	Cooperative Learning	Language Arts
Accesses information efficiently and effectively	Finds required information from a variety of sources	Contributes to team research	Follows and provides clear instructions
Evaluates information critically and competently	Validates sources; organizes and retains discovered sources	Reviews team discovered sources	Reviews and contributions are clearly communicated
Uses information effectively and creatively	Can present as text, graphics, multi-media, or hypermedia as needed	Contributes to and reviews team presentations for effectiveness	Reviews and contributions are clearly communicated
Independent Learning **	**Technology**	**Cooperative Learning**	**Language Arts**
Pursues information related to personal interests	Uses technology to create personal portfolio	Contributes resources to others, based on their interests	Personal portfolio invites and receives commentary
Appreciates literature and other creative expressions of information	Uses technology to experience and discuss all art forms	Reviews team members' cultural favorites (books, movies, music, etc.)	Reviews are clearly communicated, and receive commentary from others
Strives for excellence in information seeking and knowledge generation	Reviews of electronic sources are clear and complete	Rubric ratings of project materials are uniformly validated	Rubric rating comments are constructive and clear
Social Responsibility **	**Technology**	**Cooperative Learning**	**Language Arts**
Recognizes the importance of information to a democratic society	Portfolio contains clear personal statement on information & society	Group contributes regularly and reliably to project and school discussions	Language is clear, constructive, and responsible
Practices ethical behavior in regard to information and information technology	Observes netiquette, fair use, and other accepted norms	Guides team members toward responsible use of technology	Communications respect privacy and truthfulness
Participates effectively in groups to pursue and generate information	Regularly contributes to on-line discussions	Regularly adds to team and school databases	Uses language to encourage group achievement

* adapted from RESULTS: the key to continual school improvement, Mike Schmoker (ASCD)
**from AASL Draft standards   © Ferdi Serim, 1997

Reader Reflections

Insights: _____

_____

_____

_____

_____

_____

Actions for Our School, District, or Association To Consider: _____

_____

_____

_____

_____

_____

_____

THE ELECTRONIC ROAD AHEAD

At this total Title 1 elementary school, children flourish in a technology-infused environment.

2 Visitors to Roosevelt-Perry Elementary step into a cheerful, vibrant world the moment they enter our school. Our walls are brilliantly painted with technology themes on every door; "Voice-Activated" adorns the door of our speech teacher. A picture of a giant computer mouse announces one fourth grade classroom. Murals brighten the walls, with a full hallway scene depicting the history of communication from the hieroglyphics of the cave people to the satellite dishes of today. Our front entrance, a concrete step, is brightly painted as a 15' by 8' computer keyboard. It's perfect for children to hopscotch their names as they enter our safe and friendly school.

Technology is a recurrent theme filling every nook and cranny of Roosevelt-Perry Elementary School, and we work

JANIS LINDLEY LOWE
Roosevelt-Perry Elementary
School
Louisville, Kentucky

hard to use the technology we have well. One Tuesday a month, I offer technology in-services to teachers, who earn professional development credit by participating. We just launched a Wednesday afternoon computer class for parents. On many Thursdays, we hold Family Reading Nights, where families listen to a celebrity guest reader and use our Accelerated Reader software with their children. And those are just some of the technology activities that take place *after* school.

During school hours, Roosevelt-Perry students are using

technology in every classroom to benefit their everyday learning. In fact, when teachers visited our school as part of the annual Kentucky Education Technology Conference, they saw 25 different demonstrations of how we use technology to enhance our curriculum and manage the business of teaching. We would have showed them more except they had to go on to other parts of the conference!

There's so much to tell about how technology has benefited our school, but I would like to

Teachers at the conference saw 25 different demonstrations of how we use technology to enhance our curriculum.

concentrate on three areas: how we use it to improve reading, help teachers control their work loads, and link the school to our surrounding community.

Technology Coordinator

I'm the technology coordinator at Roosevelt-Perry Elementary School in Louisville. In a district of more than 96,000 students, our school has the distinction of being the "poorest" school in the Jefferson County Public School District and among the poorest in the entire state of Kentucky.

We are a total Title I school, with over 97 percent of our students qualifying for free or reduced lunches. The majority of our parents have not graduated from high school, and many haven't finished the 8th grade, but we are making efforts to get them more involved in their children's schooling. Out of a total of 450 students, approximately 51 percent are white and 49 percent are African-American. All of our students come from this neighborhood.

Model Technology School

Since 1984, we have strived to infuse technology into our curriculum and school activities. A federal School of Choice grant back in 1987 funded our first computer lab, as well as my position as the computer resource teacher. By 1993, the state of Kentucky had named Roosevelt-Perry a State Model Technology School.

Our current principal, John Ansman, has continued to make school technology a priority. We actively seek out grants to update our equipment, software, and expertise. Today we proudly can say we use every piece of technology we have, old and new, to maximum effect.

Equipment

Roosevelt Perry has 27 classrooms. Each has at least one old Apple IIe computer and dot matrix printer, one other "fairly old" computer (Mac Classic,

Apple II GS, Mac LC, etc.), and one newer Power Mac. Several classrooms have as many as ten computers. These computers aren't new, but the students can use the word processing programs to develop the writing portfolios that are mandatory for every fourth grade student in Kentucky.

Networks

We have two networks throughout our building: an Appletalk network and an Ethernet network connected to a T1 line (which provides high-speed Internet access). The older Appletalk network still works perfectly to "serve out" as many as 200 software titles to the classrooms. This network also carries our in-house E-mail system and allows teachers to print to laser printers in four locations throughout the building. The Ethernet network connects to all of our classroom Power Macs,

the 27 Mac 580's in our lab, and the Macs in the administrative offices, as well as several Compaq computers in various locations around the building. The T1 line allows everyone to have access to the Internet and to have "outside-the-building" E-mail accounts using Microsoft Exchange software.

Education Reform

As part of the Kentucky Education Reform Act (KERA), the state set a goal of a 6:1 pupil-to-computer ratio—with funds established for this technology push—and made a commitment to use technology efficiently at all grade levels. Under KERA, each school designs its own consolidated plan with a specific focus. A school then must show that all its activities, such as professional development and special purchases, support the goals of its plan. For the past two years, the focus of Roosevelt-Per-

ry's consolidated plan has been reading under an umbrella of technology. In other words, we focus on reading throughout the curriculum and use technology as a tool to strengthen reading skills.

When we studied our students' test scores, we realized that reading levels were affecting their scores in every subject.

When we studied our students' test scores, we realized that reading levels were affecting their scores in every subject— understanding word problems in math, content in social studies, and higher-order thinking in science. In Kentucky our students are scored on a scale of Novice-Apprentice-Proficient-Distinguished. The high majority of our students are in the Novice range in reading. Our goal by 2000 is to increase our percentage of students scoring at Proficient by 13 percent, while decreasing our Novice levels by 10 percent.

Technology as a Link to Reading

At Roosevelt-Perry, we incorporate technology to teach reading in many different ways. For example, we use word processing to teach reading through writing.

A fourth-grader who initially had no interest in reading became motivated enough to reach for harder books herself.

Students write more if they can word process rather than write and erase, write and erase. We also use multimedia reports as a tool to enhance student reading. Research projects that culminate in multimedia presentations are exciting to students and teachers. Students become more involved in the process of reading if they are creating a multimedia presentation as the end result rather than writing a five- or ten-page report.

Our school has accumulated about 300 educational software titles over the years, dating back to phonics software for our Apple IIe computers, and we still use many of them. However, one of the best reading-related titles we've acquired recently is Accelerated Reader. Students reading at a first grade level and higher use Accelerated Reader software, which tests comprehension after they have read a book. Each disk in the series includes tests for about 36 books, so we purchase the software that includes books our students are likely to read.

The Point System

I first started using the Accelerated Reader software in my Extended School Sessions (an afterschool program) last year. Students read books, took the comprehension tests, and accumulated points in a system I devised in which the kids earn more points when they read more challenging books. By the end of the year, all the students had points and could select prizes from my box of items donated by teachers. A basketball selected by Jerry, the child with the highest number of points, was a real hit. Jerry now uses Accelerated Reader to improve his reading skills in the afterschool program, in his regular classroom, and at our Family Reading Nights.

I've also had many students like Beth, a fourth grader who initially had no interest in reading. I began by handing her easy books so she could take the

Accelerated Reader tests, earn points, and feel successful. When she realized she could earn more points with more difficult books, she became motivated to reach for those harder books herself!

Reading by Grade Level

Here a few examples of how each grade in our school is using technology to bolster or augment reading:

• **Kindergarten.** Mrs. Bratcher's class, and three other kindergarten classes, use First Steps: Pictures, Letters, and Sounds from Educational Publishing Concepts. The software takes students through phonics lessons: the computer speaks out loud so the children can practice their letter sounds and blends. It is colorful, easy to use, and the children love it.

• **First Grade.** Ms. Erny's class used the Encyclopedia of Animals (now called Animal Behavior) laserdisc series to write short research papers on animals. Each child selected and wrote about an animal, then taped a pre-printed barcode to the top of his or her paper. After reading the report to the class, the student took a hand-held barcode scanner and scanned the barcode to activate the laserdisc, which in turn entertained the class with more facts and a short movie clip about the animal. What an exciting technology tool for young students!

• **Second Grade.** Mr. Connelly's class each brought in teddy bears from home. They measured the bears and collected other data about their "specimens"— for example, whether a bear was smooth or furry, how large the bear was, etc. Then they used Claris-Works (an integrated word processing, spreadsheet, database, and drawing program) to put

this information into a database. Students then searched the database to answer questions such as, "Whose bear is the smallest?"

• **Third Grade.** Mrs. King's class used HyperStudio (a multimedia authoring tool) to build a stack of informational cards for a

---

What's a Stack? How To Explain HyperStudio to Elementary Students

We frequently use HyperStudio, a multimedia authoring tool for Mac or Windows. It's easy to combine words, images, photos, and video onto electronic "cards" covering any subject. Children must research, write, create, and organize to create the cards. A collection of these cards becomes a "stack."

To introduce the concept of HyperStudio to a class of third graders, I explained a stack in terms of index cards: If you have a bunch of index cards, you can number them #1, #2, and so on. You can lay them on a table and start switching the order—for example, going from #4 to #35 and then to #17. What you're doing in HyperStudio is assembling information in your computer that is like a series of cards that can be viewed in any order. I tell them, "This is just the way your brain works, flipping from one thought to another!"

research project on animals. They learned to scan in a picture of their animal; create cards, buttons, and transitions from one card to another; and use a digital camera to show pictures of themselves working on the project for their author cards.

I show teachers how computers can help them manage their workloads.

• **Fourth Grade.** Mrs. Hollenbeck's class uses Microsoft Exchange E-mail to correspond with a U.S. Navy ship at sea. A sailor "key pal" has sent the class pictures, and their classroom wall is dedicated to messages they've exchanged and the theme of communication in general. Fourth grade students also use Claris-

Works to develop their writing portfolios and import pictures they've taken with a digital camera.

• **Fifth Grade.** Mr. Quick had students download pictures from the Internet and save them into separate photo libraries in ClarisWorks. Now when they write reports or stories, they have customized graphics to insert into their stories. Fifth grade students also spend a lot of time becoming proficient with spread sheets. We expect them to know how to create and manipulate them in order to find the speediest, most efficient route to needed information.

Our teachers are especially fond of Skills Connection, a mammoth database of standardized tests. This program enables us to create highly professional assessment tools that are uniquely tailored to our curriculum and our students' needs. Students

tell us that these standardized tests free them from the intimidation they might otherwise feel when confronting state or national assessments.

Technology as a Link to Classroom Management

In addition to helping teachers use technology to teach our kids, I show them how computers can help them manage their work loads. For example, every teacher has a $300 working budget for the year. Many now use a ClarisWorks spreadsheet to keep tabs on their purchases and their budget. No more trying to locate little receipts and wondering how much money is left as they look through a catalogue!

Another great tool for classroom management is Classroom Publisher, a program that helps teachers create seating charts, calendars, parent newsletters, place cards, greeting cards, awards, and certificates. Classroom Publisher also has eye-catching pieces of clip art appropriate for schools. I saw an advertisement for this software, and ten of our teachers decided to pool their own money to buy a ten-pack for about $390. When the other teachers saw what a useful and creative time-saver it could be, they bought copies as well.

Teachers in our district need to take 24 hours of professional development each year. I keep a database in ClarisWorks with our teachers' names, which courses or in-services they've taken, how many hours they've totaled so far, and the training they've received in a particular topic. Once a month, I teach an hour-long technology inservice. Some months we spend on hardware, such as how to connect an Apple IIe to a TV set for whole class instruction or how to use a digital camera. Other months, we spend on features that help teachers organize or conserve their time, such as using E-mail to communicate outside and inside of the school. (E-mail is a great way to avoid running across the building to tell someone something, only to find the person isn't there!) We can also use E-mail to easily access our district's central offices to get information on attendance records, professional development, purchasing, pupil personnel issues, and the dozens of other issues that can come up in the course of a day.

Electronic Road Ahead Grant
In 1996, our school won an Electronic Road Ahead grant for $30,000 from the National Foundation for the Improvement of Education, the National

Have You Ever Seen a Literacy Garden?

The entire front perimeter of our school has been divided into eleven special gardens, each based on a popular children's book. A yellow brick road winds through the *Wizard of Oz* garden. A totem pole and a 16-foot teepee stand sentinel in *the Legend of Bluebonnet* garden. A profusion of "chocolate" mint plants grow in the *Willy Wonka and the Chocolate Factory* garden. And the *Fairy Tale* garden is filled with stepping stones that look like tree trunks and "enchanted" benches in the shape of animals.

Each Literacy Garden was designed and created by one or more classes. After choosing a book and a theme for their gardens, students used the ClarisWorks drawing program to map out the design of their gardens. Then they conducted research by going online to gardening Web sites for kids. Jeanette McDermott from Learning Pursuits, Inc., served as the Scientist in Residence and coordinator for the program. All of our hard work has paid off. Our students were very excited when Roosevelt-Perry beat out 26 other schools to receive this year's Fred Wiche School Gardening Award!

Education Association, and Bill Gates of Microsoft. We became one of 22 winning sites from across the United States. Over the two years of the grant, we were able to purchase hardware, software, and many accessories (such as digital cameras, additional computer memory, Zip drives, etc.) We also trained a core group of six teachers, spread out across the grade levels, in the use of multimedia technology.

Our students designed a multimedia presentation to run in an information kiosk at the Portland Museum.

The grant served as a catalyst for our school, mainly because it resulted in a group of trained and enthusiastic teachers. I believe that what we did during the two years of the Road Ahead grant could be done by any school. Yes, you'll need funding, but much can be done on a smaller scale with one multimedia computer and a video and/or digital camera.

During the first year of the grant, fourth and fifth grade students used HyperStudio to produce electronic portfolios that contained examples of their school projects, scanned writing samples, videos of presentations and book reports, photographs, and other student-selected samples. They also learned to use a scanner, video camera, digital camera, and voice recorder. These electronic portfolios served to teach both the students and the teachers the basics of multimedia.

Technology as a Link to the Community

In the second year of the Road Ahead project, our school worked with the Portland Museum to design a multimedia presentation that would run in an information kiosk at the museum. Originally our goal was to cover Louisville architecture, schools, churches, famous people, river-based activities, the arts, and other topics. It didn't take long to figure out that we had bitten off too much content! At this point, Nathalie Andrews, executive director of the museum, suggested we concentrate on three topics:

• the old Roosevelt school built in 1866, the oldest school in our district and the predecessor of our current school.

• Henrietta Helm, an African-American teacher in the early 1900s, who became the principal of the Portland Colored Evening School, where adults learned to read at night.

• the Squire Earick house, the 12th oldest home in Louisville, which is open to the public and located in our neighborhood.

The project involved third and fourth graders, who split into three groups to do the research and create HyperStudio stacks with the information they collected.

Sharing Information

Many visitors came to share their memories from the past with the students, and we also went out into the community to explore local history. For example, Henrietta Helm's great-nephew came with books he had found in a trunk she once owned. Students gently stroked the books and carefully turned pages of history as they appreciated her beautiful penmanship, nearly a century old. We took bus trips to see the site of the Evening School. We also toured the inside of the Squire Earick house and visited the old Roosevelt School, which is currently being turned into 45 low-income apartments. The architect, Mark Bailey, came to answer questions from our students. He brought building plans and taught the students to read his architectural drawings.

With the information they had gathered from their research, the students worked together on storyboards. The storyboards were 3' by 9' pieces of cardboard, on which they could arrange and rearrange hand-designed cards to develop the flow of their presentations. In preparing their multimedia presentation for the information kiosk, students had to consider what questions a museum visitor might want answered. Once they made these decisions "on paper," each child completed from one to three HyperStudio cards that combined words, pictures, and sound.

For the sound portion of their presentation, they composed songs for each of their three research areas. Then they recorded the songs and imported the music into their presentation. At the bottom of each card is a recognition sentence for the child who made it. How proud they are when they visit the museum and see their names displayed along with their research! We also had a ribbon-cutting ceremony for parents to see their children's project.

Originally, we planned to make a CD of our presentation for the kiosk. But the only CD write-on technology we could afford made for a choppy presentation. (The technology has since improved and come down in price.) So we saved the presentation on a Zip disk (a disk that can store 100 megabytes of information or about 100 times more

Using multimedia technology as a learning tool really reinforced students' knowledge.

than a floppy disk) instead, and that is what is running in the kiosk now.

Results That Matter
We gave our students pre- and post-tests on the use of multimedia (see reproducible). Our project was inclusive of special education students, and we can

unequivocally state that every student knows the process and can quickly and easily put together a stack of information.

Using multimedia technology as a learning tool really reinforced students' knowledge. By the time they finished their stacks, they knew the content inside out! In addition, they learned technical skills they will transfer to the job world someday, they learned to work in small groups, and they had a great sense of accomplishment when everything "worked"! We teachers also learned a lot. At times, we were just a few steps ahead of the kids in figuring out how to use some of the technology.

Next Steps

As the technology coordinator for our school, I know that one of my main challenges is finding ways to update our equipment. We do have a lot of equipment, but much of it is five years or older, and the new software that is coming out needs more and more computer memory. Fortunately, our school recognizes that technology purchases are a priority. With the site-based decision making that our district practices, that means we budget the money to buy two or three new computers a year.

Overall, I feel very hopeful about the future. The Kentucky Education Reform Act emphasizes hands-on discovery, real-life application, student research, and the use of computers as a learning tool. At Roosevelt-Perry, we've managed to offer an exciting, technology-infused education that sets our students on the road to a bright future.

Multimedia Pre-Test and Post-Test for Elementary Students

Name _____

Look at the paper you have been given.

1. This is a picture of a:
   a. card   c. stack
   b. picture   d. I don't know

2. Look at the picture of your teacher. How did that get in the computer? Explain.
   a. It was scanned in from a picture.
   b. It was taken by a xap shot camera.
   c. I don't know.

3. Look at the #4 on the paper. What is it pointing to?
   a. a stack   c. a card
   b. a button

4. Have you ever made a HyperStudio stack of information? yes no

5. Have you ever used a xap shot camera? yes no

6. Have you ever used a scanner? yes no

7. What color is the background on this example?

8. Why is there a picture of a little house in the bottom left corner?

9. What does a scanner do? Explain how to use it.

10. Name three visual effects you could choose as a transition from one card to another.

11. Look at the paper. Why is there a vertical gray area on the right side of the words? What is it called?

12. What is a font? Look at the word "Artist." Do you think it is a 9 point or 24 point font? Explain.

13. On the back of this paper, explain what a HyperStudio stack is and how you make one. Tell everything you know.

Helpful Hints for Using Technology In Your Classroom

- Buy a manual at a bookstore. Multiple computer purchases often don't include enough manuals. Share the cost with a fellow teacher or try to get reimbursed by your school.

- Learn one new trick each day. Keep a manual handy and read just two paragraphs each day. Team up with another teacher and challenge each other.

- Teach the entire class from one computer. An old Apple IIe will easily connect to a TV set. A card can be installed inside a Macintosh so that you can project it to a large screen or LCD panel. If you don't have a large pull-down screen, buy foamboard, tape it together, and set it on your chalk ledge.

- Include at least one technology goal on your annual growth plan. Then do it.

- Clean up your computer area. It's not inviting when there are dust balls around the computer and the keyboard is dirty. One child and a box of Q-tips can do wonders. Kids think it's fun!

Reader Reflections

Insights: _____

_____

_____

_____

_____

_____

Actions for Our School, District, or Association To Consider: _____

_____

_____

_____

_____

_____

A GLOBAL LINK TO LANGUAGES

For students in this Spanish class, the Internet provides a cultural immersion difficult to come by in their rural community.

3

If I am teaching in five years the way I'm teaching today, I should not be teaching at all.

This has been my credo since I began teaching Spanish in Charles City, Iowa, in 1967. Almost 30 years later, when I got my first glimpse of the Internet at a conference in the early 1990s, I knew that my teaching would change forever. Foreign language education, E-mail, and the World Wide Web are a perfect fit, because language and the new technology are all about communications.

I teach high school in Charles City, a largely rural school district in northeast Iowa. In the late 1980s, our community was hard hit by the collapse of its largest industry, a tractor factory—a blow that followed by only a few years a devastating tornado that had leveled three schools, as well as the downtown area. The population losses resulting from

these calamities drastically reduced student enrollment and forced the school district to downsize staff and programs. Since the 1970s, our student population has shrunk from about 3,000 students to fewer than 2,000.

Well over 60 percent of our students are enrolled for two years in German or Spanish. Anyone who has ever studied a foreign language knows that cultural and linguistic immersion is the best way to master a new tongue, and such immersion has often been difficult to provide. For my students in rural Iowa,

AL BODE

Charles City High School

Charles City, Iowa

the Internet provides cultural and linguistic immersion that would otherwise be nearly impossible for us to come by.

My students don't learn in a traditional classroom setting. They enter a room in which eight movable couches form a ring around a wide carpeted open area in the center. There

Because of technology, I've become more of a guide and motivator in the education process.

are no "back seats," so everyone must participate. Advanced students work with lower level students to encourage the best oral and written performance possible. At times, an assortment of teenagers will be found using white pared down shower-board sheets to practice writing in Spanish, while a radio station

from Guadalajara or Merida plays in the background. Some of the third- and fourth-year students may be communicating in Spanish via E-mail with class-rooms in an adjacent county or even on an adjacent continent. One or two may be utilizing the Web to learn more about Puerto Rico. Still others may be reading the daily news in Spanish in *El Diario* from Yucatan.

From Dictator to Motivator

Whether my students are reading the Yucatan daily newspaper on-line or writing E-mail to pen pals in Montevideo or San Juan, they're having a learning experience they can't get from a text-book. And mainly because of the world that is now open to them via technology, I have become a guide and motivator instead of a dictator in the education process.

It's been a long journey from prescriptive teaching to guiding student learning. Having been inspired by my own high school Spanish teacher in rural Iowa, I had decided early to become a teacher of Spanish. During my first 10 years of teaching I attempted, as did many other foreign language teachers in the U.S., to infuse language-lab tech-nology and learning packets into a textbook-driven curriculum. My students achieved ade-quately, but I was bothered by enrollment declines after the second-year Spanish classes. Al-though students' full schedules appeared to be the problem, I felt that the lab drills and lock-step textbooks were discouraging them from going on to a third and fourth year of language study.

I worked hard to find ways to create a more motivational framework for students. In pursuit of this goal, I began a two-pronged transformation of my classroom that still continues 22 years later. First, I started writing my own curriculum from scratch, with study materials, which I continue to revise each year in lieu of textbooks and workbooks. Second, I made the classroom more homelike and non-threatening. I sought to re-create the kind of environment in which young people had learned their first language. With my students' help, and castoff furniture and carpets from the community, I created a "living room" in which learning could take place comfortably and more effectively than in a regimented classroom.

By the 1980s, I had introduced technology to my classes. Recognizing the potential for computers in assisting instruction, I had purchased a small TI-99 4A personal computer and, using Basic language, had developed various practice and enrichment programs, which included creating one with letters and diacritical marks needed in writing Spanish. In 1985, I bought a KAYPRO-2X with Spanish and English keyboards, a word processing capacity in both languages, and sufficient memory to store student work and curriculum rewrites. This was replaced in 1993 by the Macintosh and IBM-compatible computers currently available for student use in my classroom.

A Leap Forward

The year 1993 also marked the beginning of a leap forward in my thinking about technology. Until 1992, I had taught Spanish to both elementary and high school students. My Spanish-FLEX (exploratory) program for fourth-graders was designed to diminish the language-learning anxiety so often experienced in middle and high school introductory courses. The inclusion of culture-based activities seemed to motivate students to continue Spanish in middle and high school, and I designed a fourth-through-twelfth grade program for school board consideration. Although the elementary program fell victim to the downsizing of the early 1990s, technological integration began to flourish.

By 1994, I had become an advocate for expanding distance learning through the Iowa Communications Network (ICN) that serves all 99 counties and all school districts in Iowa. As a result of my involvement with ICN, I was invited to attend the Secretary's Conference on Educational Technology in Washington, D.C. At the meeting, I became entranced by a demonstration in which people were communicating with one of the presenters—face-to-face, from all over the world—through her computer. That day I discovered the power of the Internet. Life in my classroom would never be the same again.

To have this constant and remarkable link to other countries

The cost for providing my classroom with this learning tool was far above my meager budget.

and cultures right in our own classroom became an all-consuming goal for me. But the cost for providing my classroom with this learning tool was far above my meager budget. The single Internet-connected computer provided through a grant to the science department was the only available connection in the school.

Getting Grant Funding

I knew one path to greater Net accessibility might be through the Roy J. Carver Trust, a fund that annually awards grants to Iowa school districts to transform the traditional classroom experience. As a member of our school's grant-writing team, I saw the possibility of obtaining a grant for installing the Internet in the district's five schools (one high school, one middle school, and three elementary). Funding from the Carver Trust might also enable us to join the International Education and Resource Network (I*EARN), an organization that matched U.S. schools with overseas partners. My aim was to establish an E-mail link with a Spanish-speaking country in South America.

Our Proposal

The format for our communications plan was established in the proposal we submitted to the

Carver Trust. Beyond the initial goal of connecting all district schools via cable television facilities, the remaining goals applied exclusively to the Spanish program. We stated that we intended "to foster a knowledge of the Internet/E-mail systems as a prerequisite to national/international communications." Second, we would shift the focus from language as the content of instruction to language as a means to access another culture and foster global understanding. The final goal was to develop joint projects with schools in Spanish-speaking countries as a means of understanding other cultures.

In response to our proposal, we received from the Carver Trust one of its largest grants for the 1995-96 school year. Then, through the initiative of the technology coordinator and a small group of determined teachers, we wired classrooms in all the buildings to cut the costs of the electrical work.

Contact!

From I*EARN, we learned of schools overseas willing to be partners in a communications project such as we envisioned. We soon established communications with two schools in Uruguay, one in Argentina, and one in Mexico City. The most promising contact was a "plantel," a high school allied with the National Autonomous University of Mexico (UNAM) in Mexico City. With that partnership, the idea of actually communicating face-to-face began to pick up steam.

Since they were as yet unable to create their own E-mail accounts in 1995, my third- and fourth-year students began to pave the way for Internet communication by developing "culture packages" to be sent to each overseas school. The packages contained items (for example, a pop recording or a photo from a school sporting event) intended to convey the flavor of our culture. We documented, by video and still camera, the selection and packing of the "cultural memorabilia" we sent to other countries. And we arranged for similar documentation when one Uruguayan school and the Mexico City plantel reciprocated with culture packages of their own. Global communication was underway.

The packages became the stimuli for student communications that would expand with our Internet connection. My students wanted to know more about "Day of the Dead" poems sent to them from Mexico City, along with candy skulls and bright tissue paper cutouts. Although the culture exchanges have now been superseded by the joint projects we conduct via the Web, they were an exciting adjunct to our early experience with the Internet.

In our first tries at communicating across borders via the Internet, we experienced some disappointments. For instance, in March 1996, an attempt at a video-conferencing session between our classroom and UNAM through CU-SeeMe software,

In response to our proposal, we received one of the largest grants for the school year.

though a visual success, was an audio disaster. We couldn't hear anything! We are still working to perfect our communications channels by, among other things, trying to find software that will enable us to hold video conferences more effectively with partners in Latin America.

After the Carver grant got us started, my students were

especially eager to create their own Web pages. After reading numerous articles and exchanging E-mail with other teachers about protection for students on the Internet, I felt that each student should limit his or her information to a first name, Spanish course name, and a picture. Each item required parental approval, as well as conformity to our district's acceptable use policy, which spells out student behavior on the Internet and in E-mail.

Once the protocols were set, it was time for the students to learn how to create their Web pages. (At that time it was still necessary for users to learn hypertext mark-up language—HTML—to create Web pages.) When they had written the basic information to be placed on their Web pages, had taken their pictures with a Flex-Camera, and had incorporated backgrounds, they had to make sure their pages were properly linked to the main student home page for the school. All this meant an expansion of their knowledge of technology, which would give them some preparation for their future academic and career undertakings.

That was our beginning. The scope of our technology initiatives can be gleaned from our Foreign Language Web site, which has received a Showcase Award given through a state educational consortium.

The Ever-Expanding Spanish Web Site

Our Web site (www.charles-city.k12.ia.us/bode/quickindex.html) contains unique materials created for student use, in addition to over 110 major links to resources for teachers and students of foreign language. It also contains information that enables parents and other family members to become involved in what is happening in their children's Spanish class. The Internet, especially when it is accessible in a student's home, makes schoolwork meaningful to parents and helps enlist their support with homework and other class-related activities.

Our ever-expanding Web site contains most of the written materials presented in first- and second-year classes. Placing our classroom materials on-line allows the students and parents to check weekly and monthly calendars for dates of tests and due-dates for homework. They can also explore other foreign language-oriented sites.

Anyone who has visited a large interactive instructional Web site knows the range and variety of information and the capacity for access is almost unlimited. Some of the highlights of our site are:

The Quick Index Page

The starting point for our foreign language Web site, the Quick Index Page, was created to enable rapid access into our Spanish program for students, parents, and other community members. The page is learner-friendly, enabling other educators to borrow our materials or page formats. We welcome other students and educators to link to our pages, which are updated regularly and which are linked to 110 other sites.

Global Identification Units

For our second-year students, identification—by sight—of all the countries in the world is essential for passing Spanish. Geography study in Spanish reinforces social studies content from other English-language classes. In addition, our global identification units, created with HyperStudio, enable students to identify all countries and capitals in the world, as well as the nationalities and the languages spoken in each country. The pages in this area are made interactive through an image-mapping process that allows a user to click on any part of a graphic to locate additional information. Specific parts of each area are invisibly "mapped" to yield more information.

Web Quest

A Web Quest developed for Charles City and San Juan students can be utilized by other schools in the United States in cooperation with Puerto Rican schools. Our Web Quest is a bilingual teaching aid designed to foster in-depth study of issues by demanding that students use a multitude of resources that offer different perspectives on an

Our Web site helps make students' schoolwork more meaningful and accessible to parents.

issue. Through Web Quest, for example, students have access to the full range of opinions on the issue of possible statehood for Puerto Rico

Interactive Writing Pages

These pages enable students to practice writing and spelling items as much as they want and to compare their practice with correctly spelled items on the Web (see reproducible). Overall written performance among first-year students has improved

Overall written performance has improved because of interactive Web pages.

markedly because of this interactive feature that can be used either in the classroom or at home. Vocabulary is also placed on interactive pages for comparison, a presentation that is similar to, but more effective than, flash cards.

Carver Grant Information and Other Assistance
I've included information about the Carver Grant and a copy of our grant proposal on our site to help other communities begin to focus on technology as a tool

rather than as a separate discipline. Also included on this section are links to the design for our Information Resource Center at the high school and the Wide Area Network (WAN) for the schools in general. To promote usage of the video-interactive classrooms on the ICN by other foreign language programs in Iowa, a "Scheduling Made Easy" page is provided. And there is even a page to assist teachers and students in creating their own Web pages!

Other Links
Although we are not currently members of I*EARN, we maintain a link for others who would consider using this organization as a starting point for international communications. There is also a link to FLTEACH, the foremost foreign language listserv for foreign language teachers.

Scattered throughout the Quick Index page are links to our

main foreign language treasure trove: the Quick Foreign Language Links index. Here teachers can link to on-line Spanish radio stations and hundreds of foreign language newspapers. An Intercambio (exchange) link provides ample school sites for exchanging E-mail and for formalized information. These are ever-expanding sections and although only created in August 1998, they have steadily become key national and international resource sites.

Reaching Our Goals
In the years since the decision to apply for the Carver Grant, we have not achieved all our goals. But technology is ever-changing, ever-enabling. All schools in our district are beginning to utilize the Internet as a tool in their curricula. I have yet to be able to teach from one building to another, but I am able to conduct inservice sessions on utilizing

technology in foreign language learning from our video-interactive site in Charles City to other sites across the state. An adjunct of the Carver Grant is the establishment of a community access room for the local cable company that provides intra-school links. These links may mean that I'll once again be able to teach elementary students.

Doorway to Global Citizenship

My teaching style has changed dramatically as the result of computer technology. And I believe that my wired, interactive, globally linked classroom offers evidence of technology's potential to make the study of Spanish a dynamic, living, social experience. My students understand that Spanish is not just a course in high school, but rather the doorway to global citizenship. Parents and administrators know that the Web is expanding students' horizons and enlarging their world.

Our Web site not only makes us citizens of a world community—it brings us closer to our home community. We have made our Web site a community resource. Technology is improving our communication with neighbors around the globe. Just as important, it's improving our communication with neighbors down the street.

I've found that with the help of computer technology, each Spanish class becomes a family in and of itself. And the friendship and trust that develops among the students in the classroom and among their international counterparts outlasts the classroom activity. My goal in teaching language— in teaching the art of communication—is and has always been a simple one: to enhance the understanding that peace within the human family begins with active respect for the language and culture of others. Technology offers us the opportunity to deepen and expand this respect.

Writing on the Web

Students can use interactive pages like the one below to practice writing and spelling Spanish.

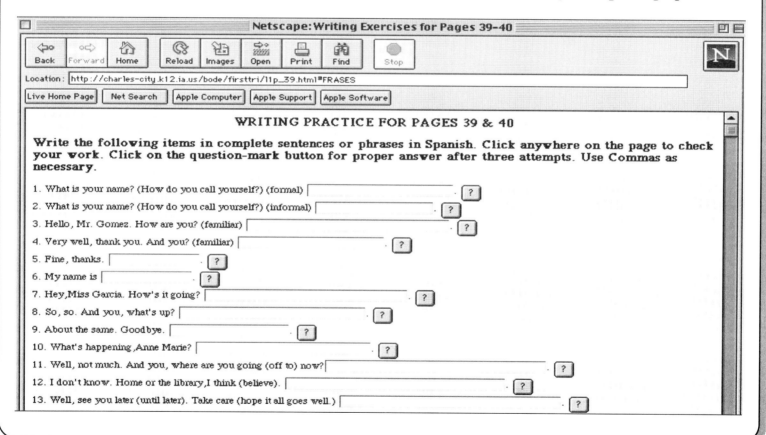

Insights: _____

_____

_____

_____

_____

_____

Actions for Our School, District, or Association To Consider: _____

_____

_____

_____

_____

_____

_____

FROM CARD FILE TO TECHNO FILE

This librarian turned media specialist helps teachers use technology to revamp traditional instruction and revitalize the curriculum.

4 The transformation from a traditional school librarian to a Library/Media Specialist has been a long, sometimes painful, often challenging experience. But as I now watch elementary school students producing multimedia presentations, designing Web pages, and surfing the Net to conduct research, I'm very glad I hung in there and completed the journey from card file to "technophile."

I've held the position of the Library/Media Specialist at Waggoner Elementary School for nearly 18 years. During that time, the K-5 population has jumped from fewer than 500 to more than 670 students. Most of this growth is recent and has sent the district hurrying to counter the threat of overcrowding. Kyrene School District has built one or two schools every year for several years, so most schools are new, although Waggoner is among the oldest. Built in the 1960s, it was "made new" three years ago through extensive remodeling. There were also additions, most notably my home base—a beautiful library resource center.

Located southeast of the Phoenix metropolitan area, Waggoner School is one of 17 elementary schools in the Kyrene District. There are also six middle schools, which feed into three high schools that are located outside our district. The area

ELAINE SNIDER

Waggoner Elementary School

Tempe, Arizona

is largely suburban, having developed from a mostly rural part of our valley. The district remains predominantly middle class and white, though we do have a growing Hispanic population.

The Waggoner staff is close, cohesive, and team-oriented. All of us collaborate on a School

A colleague of mine later observed that we were in effect using a nuclear reactor to power a rowboat.

Improvement Plan that targets the areas we deem most in need of improvement and most deserving of concentrated focus. Our current plan specifies the need to ensure that all of our students are comfortable with technology and equipped with the skills they'll need to keep expanding their technological know-how.

A Traditional Librarian Meets Technology

My first encounter with classroom technology came in 1985 when we installed the Follett Circulation Program on Apple IIe computers in our libraries. This simple program, which helped us track the use of library materials, didn't exactly catapult us into the information age. We still used a card catalog, and I was still conducting traditional classes focusing on traditional library skills.

Very soon afterward, however, more computers were installed in schools throughout the district. Waggoner had a lab of 20-plus Apple IIe computers that we networked locally using a system purchased with donations from parents. Though we had the tools of the future, we remained pretty much wed to the past. We used new high-tech software for low-tech purposes, mainly for drill and practice. A

colleague of mine later observed that we were in effect using a nuclear reactor to power a rowboat. That's a bit strong, but the fact is that like many schools, we did not at first use the new technology to create a new curriculum. We used it to help a bit with the old curriculum.

Research tells us that this tendency to merely append technology to the traditional curriculum remains a problem in far too many schools. At Waggoner, we quickly moved beyond this syndrome. And I'm proud of the fact that I helped us get past the stage where our on-site computers were more like toys than instruments to transform instruction and revamp the curriculum.

Despite our new, well-equipped computer lab, I still knew very little about how computers worked or what they could do. Since there was a Macintosh Classic in the library that was almost never used, I decided to take a few introductory courses in basic computing.

Love at First Byte

I had no way of knowing what was in store for me. My first formal introduction to the Macintosh hooked me. Completely! I learned to love the Mac and started to use it for more and more projects. I soon realized that this machine demanded an end to business as usual. We had to find ways to use computers to revitalize learning and reinvigorate the curriculum. I was by no means a computer expert, but I knew that I wanted to be part of the process of figuring out how to harness the power of computers to improve learning.

It was at this point that I became disillusioned with teaching isolated library skills (like how to use the card catalogue) on a tight, predetermined schedule. It struck me that these sessions—like my wonderfully engineered hands-on class on using an encyclopedia—didn't do much to improve students' skills. I had also recently begun reading about flexible library scheduling and "point of need" teaching of skills. The idea of teaching students a skill—like the use of an encyclopedia—at a time when they were actually going to need that skill to prepare a report made a lot of sense to me. It was time for some changes.

I asked Sheila Spinn, my principal at that time, for permission to have a flexible library schedule that I would use to help teachers and their students on an "as needed" basis. She agreed. The next step was to add technology to the mix, but I wasn't sure I was ready. Fortunately a colleague, third-grade teacher Jay Wallace, gave me a shove.

The Courage To Experiment

When it came to technology, Jay was fearless. He wanted to experiment with computers and enlisted my help so he could take advantage of the four new AV-capable computers and the scanner we now had in the library.

Jay and I started helping students prepare PowerPoint presentations, scan pictures for

We had to find ways to use computers to revitalize learning and reinvigorate the curriculum.

incorporation into their reports, use word-processing applications, and even add movie clips to presentations. We weren't always sure about how to do everything, but we learned from our mistakes. And we kept

Organizing a Volunteer Work Force

Parents are our most valuable allies. And they can be a terrific resource if they see the value of the work you're doing. Here are a few tips for helping you organize parents—and grandparents—into a volunteer work force.

- Work closely—and respectfully—with a parent or grandparent who is willing to serve as the *coordinator of volunteers*. Placing this responsibility in someone else's hands will ease the burden on you and will also foster a spirit of teamwork among volunteers.

- Let volunteers know that you really need them and that their efforts are essential to the goal of *improved student achievement*.

- Give volunteers a detailed, long-range schedule. Volunteers are most reliable when they are able to *plan ahead*.

- Don't treat volunteers as volunteers, but as valued and trusted members of a work force. Be sure to emphasize that all work is *on behalf of the students*.

- Encourage your students to express their *gratitude* to volunteers.

plugging away until we got the results we wanted. I loved learning how to produce multimedia, and it was thrilling to see how motivating this was for students. Our first full-fledged project was a unit on dinosaurs that lasted almost all year!

Staff Support

The time had come to persuade the rest of the staff that we needed a schoolwide commitment to integrating technology into the curriculum. I approached the faculty as a whole at a staff meeting. I showed them the PowerPoint presentations and the other computer-based projects that Jay and I had done with his students. I also pulled in some parents and showed them the work students were doing in the library and computer lab. The parents' enthusiasm helped build momentum for introducing more technology into the curriculum.

Excitement about "technologizing" the curriculum grew quickly. A sure sign of this enthusiasm was our staff's decision to endure slightly larger class sizes in order to fund a half-time position for a master technology teacher. We were determined to prepare students for a future that would be increasingly technology-dependent.

Jay Wallace assumed the position of master technology teacher, job sharing his third-grade class so that he could devote half his time to the computer lab. He and I began to work even more closely together, and our collaboration continues today. With Jay in the lab and with the help of library/media technician Charlene Holbein as well as a dedicated group of parent and grandparent volunteers, I'm able to devote myself fully to helping teachers integrate technology into their curricular areas. My technology-laden library/resource program would also not be possible without my principal, Julie Weimer, who has offered spirited support to the ideal that students and teachers ought to learn technology together.

Beefing Up Technology

One of the biggest challenges to using technology with maximum effectiveness at Waggoner has been the lack of equipment that is powerful enough to support widespread use of memory-consuming and space-consuming software. A parent's generous donation of eight iMac computers for our lab has gone a long way toward alleviating this problem. In addition, our citizen's bond committee has recommended that the school board release $4.1 million to expand and upgrade technology throughout the district. This will most certainly help solve our hardware problems.

Our lab now has 29 computers (all connected to the Internet), a networked Laser printer, and three stand-alone color printers. Students also have access to a scanner and a digital camera. We link our computers together in a LAN (local area network) within each school and also in a WAN (wide area network) that connects all district schools to each other, to the district office, and to a central server site that provides Internet access without need for a dial-up service.

Technology Targets

Our district-wide technology plan includes targets for each grade level. While our district technology director, Mada Kay Moorehead, was very active in developing the plan, she lets us decide how we are going to meet grade-level goals. Jay and I are really happy that we have that freedom. We are able to ensure that the needs of staff and students, rather than software applications, drive integration of technology into the curriculum. The following grade-by-grade account of our students' technology activities suggests a typical curricular sequence. But we're flexible about what skills are taught and when they are introduced.

• **Kindergarten:** Students begin to learn keyboarding, basic computer operations, and appropriate terminology. We use verbal quizzes to help guide

Our principal supports the ideal that students and staff should learn technology together.

them through this introductory material. We also give the students plenty of time to work with KidPix, a multimedia program that includes a mini-word processor and a graphics program.

• **First grade:** Students focus on computer operations. Using KidPix, they write a sentence, illustrate it with the program's drawing tools, and then record their voices "narrating" the sentence. We then put each student's work into a slide show for the entire class to view.

• **Second grade:** Students focus on problem-solving skills and begin to learn the process of navigating a program or site. We

The Internet really pumps up students' enthusiasm for learning about computers.

use HyperStudio, a multimedia program that helps students understand links, superlinks, and how to present information in a logical sequence. Some of the buttons/links trigger voice recordings or animations. We have students develop an electronic portfolio of their school experiences. These multimedia portfolios typically include photographs, a voice recording, perhaps even a passage from a student's favorite book. When parents come to school for a conference, students lead them through a tour of their portfolios.

• **Third grade:** Students begin to use technology as a research tool and to create more elaborate products like book reports. They also start using the Internet, an activity that really pumps up their enthusiasm for learning everything they can about computers. Students use HyperStudio, as well as clip art programs and scanners, as a means of organizing and demonstrating the results of their research on the Net.

• **Fourth grade:** Students continue to use technology as a research tool. We increase the time they spend on the Internet and help them learn the most efficient ways to navigate the World Wide Web. All fourth-graders use the Web sites to study the history, geography, and economy of Arizona. One of our fourth-grade teachers, Gary Graham, encourages his students to combine the use of print material, the Internet, and both on-line and CD-ROM encyclopedias to research the state's ghost towns.

• **Fifth grade:** Students fine-tune their research skills and complete a major final product that requires use of all the computer skills they've acquired during their years at Waggoner. These are almost always multimedia products. One class, for example, produced "living books" for the kindergarten students at our school.

The students researched this project by looking at popular picture books to get ideas about the best way to organize and illustrate their own books. They used storyboards to plan and organize their HyperStudio stacks.

They made their characters talk by creating computer links that triggered a recording of their own voices as the characters, and they made objects move by creating links to animations. They used computer graphics programs to draw most of their own pictures, although some of them did import clip art from other sources. These books now reside on a computer in the library for younger students to enjoy.

Technology Brings Social Studies to Life

When I asked fifth-grade teacher, Jan Turkevich, if she would be willing to bring her kids to the library and the production lab once or twice a week to work on a unit to integrate technology and social studies, she jumped at the opportunity. Jan saw this as an ideal way to deepen her students' understanding of our Revolutionary War.

Our study stretched from September to April. We emphasized cooperative learning, a concept to which the entire Waggoner staff is committed. Jan scheduled several hours each week for her students to work with Jay and me and to make full use of the Internet, CD-ROM resources, and on-line encyclopedias.

Jan also managed to build math into her social studies unit. We first used the Internet to access the Williamsburg site and study Colonial-period buildings, then had the students determine how to make models of the buildings to scale. We used Microsoft Excel, a program that manages data and creates spreadsheets and charts, to graph the number of soldiers lost on each side during the Revolutionary War.

Students used library time to put together the materials they collected on the colonies and to develop a rough draft of what would eventually be a major report. They next came to the production lab where they put the material together on Web pages they created using Netscape Composer and HyperStudio. We considered this study complete when the students had created a multi-page Web site on the Revolutionary War.

Kids love technology—in large part because it makes them active learners.

Technology Motivates

Teachers are finding that students who were not previously motivated to do good work—or *any work*—now produce impressive and creative reports and presentations. The computer appears to energize students. And access to on-line resources has a really positive impact on students' study habits. They are much more focused and do a better job researching, especially for their age level. Kids love technology—in large part, I

The Internet increases, rather than diminishes, the need for critical thinking.

think, because it makes them active learners and increases their opportunities to experience success. I've never seen a more motivational tool.

Beyond Computer Worship

As a librarian, I've always felt that an important part of my job is helping students find information. I also feel, however, that I have a responsibility to help them interpret this information, evaluate its usefulness, and assess its accuracy. This is *especially* true in the information age.

When my students do research on the Internet, I tell them to look at as many sources as possible and then compare what they find. We must take care to see that our students understand that the presence of "information" on the Internet doesn't make it true. It needs to be checked and re-checked—often with the use of print material. I am, after all, a librarian. I want students to know that you never lose the need to use some of those traditional methods. I certainly don't hesitate to tell them that the Internet is not always the best place to find information. And what is found there must be critically evaluated. Our students learn that the Internet increases, rather than diminishes, the need for critical thinking.

At Waggoner, we're teaching our students to become independent lifelong learners. Computers may be a powerful tool, but the "engines" that drive the tool are the students themselves—their hard work, their intelligence, and their creativity. Yes, we'll continue to ensure that every student at Waggoner is technologically competent, and more important, is able to use computer technology to support and enhance their learning. But, we also want them to know that a computer, like all tools, is only as reliable as the person who uses it!

Creating a Culture of Collaboration that Supports the Use of Technology: Steps the Library/Media Specialist Can Take

- Invite one or more teachers to work with you in developing a unit of study that makes full use of the school's technology resources.

- If tightly scheduled classes create a problem, explore with the principal and other staff the possibility of introducing more flexible scheduling.

- Learn as much as possible not only about the technology at your school site, but about additional technology resources that may be available within your community.

- Serve as a role model for both students and staff by pairing up with a teacher who loves technology. Plan activities and projects that you can share with students, colleagues, and parents.

- Make use of the growing body of literature on classroom technology. Stay especially alert for articles describing activities designed to make students and teachers more comfortable with technology.

- Attend workshops whenever possible. This is a wonderful way to learn what other Library/Media Specialists are doing and what kind of programs they've developed.

- Use the Internet to stay current with innovative technology programs.

- Be patient. The successful integration of technology into the curriculum does not happen overnight. You have to willing to be disappointed and even frustrated at times. Hang in there, hang tough, hang together.

Helpful Web Addresses

http://www.techline.com/~tmallory/BER

Tia Mallory has a very helpful homepage. This is especially good for anyone hoping to find ideas for projects on the internet. She also conducts a very worthwhile workshop through BER (Bureau of Educational Research).

http://www.kyrene.k12.az.us/

This is the Kyrene School District home page. Several of the schools have pages with links to all kinds of different areas.

http://www.kyrene.k12.az.us/schools/waggoner/Waggoner.htm

This is Waggoner's home page.

http://www.kyrene.k12.az.us/schools/waggoner/Snider/esindex.html

This is my personal home page. From here, you can easily get to the pages I created about the role of a Library/Media Specialist.

esnide@wag1.kyrene.k12.az.us

This is my E-mail at school. Love to hear from you!

Reader Reflections

Insights: _____

_____

_____

_____

_____

_____

Actions for Our School, District, or Association To Consider: _____

_____

_____

_____

_____

_____

_____

WIRED FOR BETTER WRITING

Computer technology has dramatically increased the level of effort these eighth grade students put into their writing.

5 Seven short years ago, turning on a computer was a terrifying experience for me. Today, personal computers and the Internet are critical to the way I teach eighth grade English. They have also dramatically increased the level of effort my students put into their writing, which now enjoys, thanks to the Internet, a national—indeed an international—audience. The integration of technology into my teaching not only helps my students master basic English skills, it also expands their horizons and prepares them to function effectively in the information age.

For over 25 years, I've taught English to eighth graders in the Mankato area of Minnesota, the state's south central economic center. Mankato is a middle-class community of 31,000 with a minority population that is less than five percent. Most of our students continue their education beyond high school. Before 1993, I taught at Mankato West High School, where overcrowding provided the impetus to develop a separate middle school for grades seven and eight.

The use of personal computer technology is one of the distinguishing features that grew out of the planning effort for Dakota Meadows Middle School. Our broad-based planning team of teachers, administrators, and community members also opted for a "house" system, strong

BETH CRISTENSEN
Dakota Meadows Middle
School
North Mankato, Minnesota

student/faculty advisor relationships, and an emphasis on learning by doing.

Our school is organized into "houses" that are named after

We underestimated the constant demand that computer technology creates for cash.

Native American trails. I teach English to the 160 students in the Minneopa House. The purpose of our houses is to provide the intimate learning environment of small schools within our larger school. The Native American names reflect the importance of the Native American tradition to our school and community.

In the late 1980s, while Dakota Meadows was being planned, personal computers began to dot the workplace, and we knew it was only a matter of time before

parents and students would expect computers in the schools. After visiting other new schools, the planning team made a commitment to integrate computer technology into the school from the start. Fiscal tradeoffs were, of course, necessary. The physical plant was scaled back to shift money into wiring the school for the future. We chose cyberspace over physical space, opting for televisions and at least one computer in each classroom.

In the Beginning
We started small, with one computer lab and high hopes for more. But we underestimated the constant demand that computer technology creates for cash. Web sites require increased memory, and new software programs require increased speed. So upgrading computers is a frequent necessity. Fortunately, support from parents has made it possible for our school to sustain a

commitment to technology despite fluctuating budgets. We depend on money raised by our parent-teacher organization's annual magazine sale to supplement whatever funds the school district provides. We now have two computer labs connected to the Internet, one of which is equipped with the versatile Macintosh G3s. We also have two word-processing labs and a computer in every classroom.

The integration of technology into our school created two formidable challenges. One, finding enough cash for our technology needs, will always be with us. The other, bringing our faculty and staff into the information age, we have successfully overcome.

When our new school first opened, there were people who said, "I'll never, never use a computer." And there were some who dragged their feet the first year. But there's not a person now who's not computer-competent. Anyone who works in our building in any capacity—teachers, aides, cooks, janitors, electricians, full- or part-time—has an E-mail account. And anyone who works full-time has his or her own computer. Our principal uses E-mail to communicate with teachers. Faculty circulate, via E-mail, the "minutes" from house meetings to appropriate colleagues. And every year, all of us use E-mail more and more to communicate with parents. There are real advantages to being able to contact parents without the hassle of finding the right time for a telephone call.

My Personal Technology Odyssey

In 1992, I wrote a grant for my first computer. I tried to think of it as no more than a sophisticated typewriter. But when it arrived, I was so afraid that I didn't even hook it up. My nine-year-old daughter did!

Libby taught me how to use the computer at home. She was also my tutor during the six-week computer training course for district teachers in our area. Every week, on the afternoon of the course, I picked Libby up from elementary school and brought her with me. And with her help, I learned to use and appreciate computers. The classes I teach now have more technology-based projects than other classes in our school.

My daughter not only taught me how to use a computer, she also changed my life and the lives of my students. She's my favorite teacher.

Wired Students

Like my daughter, most of our students enter middle school with computer experience. Eighty percent of my students have computers in their homes.

Not all are Internet-connected, but parents often take their children to the library to do Net research. And many parents have access to the Internet and E-mail at work.

Anyone who works in our building in any capacity has an E-mail account.

Despite their level of computer experience, every student takes a self-paced, six-week keyboarding course in seventh grade. The course teaches the word processing program, ClarisWorks, to all students and gives those who already know keyboarding the opportunity to further develop their skills.

Computers and Eighth Grade English

New Routes to Old Goals
There's a reassuring constancy to the goals in eighth grade English.

Regardless of what social and economic changes sweep our world, students will always need to read skillfully, write clearly, and think critically. Technology doesn't change these goals. It simply changes the way we approach them. Computers offer students new pathways—more exciting, "traveler-friendly" routes—to the goals that I've always set for my eighth grade English classes.

Susan Eloise Hinton's novel, *The Outsiders*, has been part of my curriculum for years.

With computer-enhanced instruction, I see faster progress toward reading, writing, and critical thinking skills.

And I've always asked students to choose one of the book's main characters, then create a scrapbook based on events in the life of that character that didn't occur in the book. My aim is to have students "get inside" the character and understand his or her unique viewpoint.

The Net Works!
The electronic world at their disposal enables my students to do much more ambitious projects than they could before. They have access, through the Internet, to hundreds of *Outsider* Web sites, so there's more material to fire their imaginations. These sites also give my students the opportunity to learn how other students around the country understand the characters and events in the novel. The result is students who are more highly motivated and more focused.

My students' scrapbooks, created with the PowerPoint presentation program, are more elaborate and sophisticated than anything they could produce without electronic "cutting and pasting." But more important, I find that visiting Web sites really helps students get into the novel. They're exposed to many more thought-provoking views, most of them put forth by their peers. The Net creates a community of learners. In effect, my students take part in a nationwide seminar.

Computers give a new dimension to the projects I assign. The upshot is better learning by more motivated students. With computer-enhanced instruction, I see faster progress toward the reading, writing, and critical thinking skills I expect my eighth graders to develop. The same thing happens with other old projects that I give a new-tech twist.

Mini-Mystery Home Page
For years, my students, working in pairs, have written 300- to 500-word mini-mysteries they challenge readers to solve. The

goal of this popular exercise is to develop good writing skills. Computers move students toward this goal by facilitating the editing and rewriting processes. It's just easier to correct grammar, delete mistakes, rearrange paragraphs, and fiddle with syntax when the tool bar and all its functions are never more than a mouse click away. Correcting and re-correcting a text is a lot simpler when you're dealing with light on a screen rather than ink on a page.

Because computers bring so much ease to the editing process, my students understand that *any* mistake in something they publish on the Web is inexcusable. I think this attitude—that grammatical and syntactical

Computer Usage Test

True or False   *One hundred percent is required before a user's permit will be issued.*

T ○ F ○   1. E-mail is not guaranteed to be private and others may be able to read it.

T ○ F ○   2. School rules regarding harassment do not apply to E-mail.

T ○ F ○   3. Swearing, vulgarities, or inappropriate words will result in the user losing computer privileges.

T ○ F ○   4. Messages relating to, or in support of, illegal activities will result in the person's removal from computer usage.

T ○ F ○   5. It's OK to read X-rated materials on the Web, as long as it's not during class time.

T ○ F ○   6. Vandalism, abuse, or theft of the equipment will result in the loss of computer privileges for the rest of the school year, or longer if circumstances warrant.

T ○ F ○   7. I can add programs to the machines or take programs off.

T ○ F ○   8. I may use someone else's E-mail disk if I have his/her permission.

T ○ F ○   9. Taking or destroying someone's disk will result in the loss of computer privileges.

T ○ F ○   10. I can print materials without prior permission.

T ○ F ○   11. I don't have to follow school policy if my parents give me permission to use any Web resources on a school computer.

T ○ F ○   12. It is OK to give strangers my home address or phone number on E-mail or the Web.

T ○ F ○   13. It's OK to teach other students how to hack.

T ○ F ○   14. Flaming is OK if it's sent to friends.

T ○ F ○   15. E-mail that harasses or threatens someone should be reported to the teacher.

errors are never to be tolerated—carries over to their work even when they're not using

> *The knowledge that they're writing for the whole wired world seems to make students take greater pride in their work.*

computers. And it makes them better writers.

The district media specialist and I teach the students how to set up a Web site with the ClarisWorks Home Page program. We teach them how to use the software to create links, choose fonts, download graphics, and import animated images. After I give the students guidelines telling them what elements they must include to be published on the Internet, they work at their own pace to create a Mini-Mystery Web page that combines lucid writing with inviting graphics.

Global Recognition

Our Mini-Mystery Web site is becoming increasingly popular, garnering more than 1,000 hits a month (http://www.isd77.k12.mn.us/schools/dakota/mystery/contents.html). Over a two-year period, 31,000 people have visited us. I've learned from E-mail messages that our site is a favorite for those who are learning English. The vocabulary is the right level, and readers have to complete interactive exercises in order to solve the mystery, so they're entertained while learning the language. Our reach is international: We have readers not just from every part of the United States, but from Bosnia and Japan as well!

Needless to say, this global impact has done wonders to pump up the confidence and enthusiasm of my eighth grade writers. The knowledge that they're writing for the whole wired world seems to make students take greater pride in their work. They're more conscientious. When they see sloppy writing on the web, they don't think it's cool. And they realize how much work they must do to avoid being embarrassed themselves.

Other Class Projects

The 5,000- to 6,000-word student autobiography is another one of my standard assignments that has been enhanced by technology. I've taught the unit for some 20 years because writing about themselves helps students overcome their fear of writing.

This unit also helps students expand their understanding of computer technology. Students use the software called Reunion to construct their family trees. They become proficient with scanning technology and digital cameras so they can incorporate family photos into their autobiographies. The use of graphics software enables them to further personalize their work.

The concept of tailoring your writing to a specific audience is of primary importance in this unit. Students know that the autobiographies are for their families. And they want a first-rate product. The quality of the documents that my students produce would not be possible without computer technology. Parents appreciate the professionalism of the final product. They're proud to see their family history presented in such a classy format.

Dakota Conflict Web Site

Mankato, unfortunately, is probably best known for being the site of the largest mass hanging in the United States. In 1862, the U.S. Cavalry hung 38 Native Americans who had taken part in an uprising that became known as the Dakota Conflict. This was the first of the Dakota prairie wars that ended in the massacre at Wounded Knee in South Dakota. It also led to the forcible removal of all Native Americans from southern Minnesota. For nearly 100 years, the Dakota Conflict stood as a barrier to communication between white people and Native Americans in central Minnesota.

In 1958, a spiritual and tribal leader of the Dakotas and a white Mankato businessman became friends and decided to begin the process of reconciliation. It's a continuing process that includes an annual powwow and ceremonies honoring the reconciliation. The naming of our school, which pays tribute to the Dakota nation, was also part of the healing process. The opening of the school featured a tribal elder's blessing and a performance by Dakota dancers.

CyberFair Contest

Early in the 1998-99 school year, I took one of my classes on a field trip related to the conflict. We visited museums, cemeteries, and other nearby sites. When I

> *The quality of the documents that my students produce would not be possible without computer technology.*

heard about the Global Schoolhouse CyberFair (http://www. globalschoolhouse.org) for student-created Web sites, I thought the Dakota Conflict and the reconciliation effort that followed would make ideal subject matter for a Web site we could submit to the CyberFair's historical landmark category.

The only problem—and it was a big one—was the March 31 deadline!

We were just completing the month-long autobiography project. On March 1, at the moment my students could finally take a deep breath and call this project a done deal, I gave them a choice: Work like crazy to create a Web site for the international CyberFair contest, or work on the site at a more deliberate pace and skip the contest until the next year. I told them that entering the CyberFair contest would make sense only if their commit-

We decided to work like crazy to create a Web site for the international CyberFair contest.

ment was strong. I made it plain that a "go for it" vote by a simple majority wouldn't be enough of a buy-in. We needed solidarity. After a discussion of pros and cons, more than 85 percent of the class voted to enter the contest.

And We Were Off!

We went to a Native American community about a hour from Mankato to interview tribal historians of the Dakota tribe. Students hit the Net, cemeteries, museums, and—yes—books.

Because so much had to be done so quickly, students assumed key managerial responsibilities. Nick, for example, had a study hall every day, and he became the scanner for tons of pictures and historical documents. He was our guru in that area. So if somebody asked, "Where's my picture of Henry Sibley?" Nick could say, "I've got it here on Disc 6." We called Nick the "Scan Man."

Students worked in teams to create Web pages. Linking these pages together in at least a semi-logical fashion became the class's most imposing challenge. In order to build a Web site, you need architects. And the architects need a site map—the rough equivalent of a blueprint.

Web architecture is rough going. When you have 50 different pages from 15 different teams of students, and when all pages must link in a manner that is helpful to the user of the Web site, your first map of the site will probably be of help only to people interested in becoming lost.

The students persevered.

Because of the suddenness of our decision to enter the Cyber-Fair, we had no lab time scheduled to build our Web site. This meant everything had to be done outside of normal school hours. One Saturday, I had 14 kids spending all day in the lab. And we were there until six o'clock every night after school. The architects hung in there. The Web site got built.

On March 31, our D-Day, we were still proofing copy and double-checking the links on our Web site (http://www.isd77.k12.mn.us/schools/dakota/conflict/history html). At 10:39 p.m., we officially entered the CyberFair competition. Whew!

A few weeks later, my students and I were delighted to learn that our Dakota Conflict site was one of five finalists in the historical landmark category. Then, in May, word came that we had won the grand prize in this category!

We were thrilled! And we were honored. But what matters most to all of us is that we're letting a worldwide audience know that the story of the Dakota Conflict did not end with that terrible violence in 1862. The reconciliation effort makes it a continuing, contemporary story. Because of the Internet, comput-er technology, and a group of dedicated eighth grade English students, Mankato's story will be known beyond Mankato. The story we told on the Web is the story of forgiveness and healing and understanding. It is the story of Mankato's past and of our future.

Internet Safety

Although middle school students have a strong sense of right and wrong, they often need to work on developing good judgment and a sense of responsibility. Our Internet policy, because it makes the consequences of poor choices so clear, helps students develop these virtues.

Each year, we mail copies of the school district's Internet Guidelines to students' parents or guardians. Parents must sign a document stating that they have read and discussed the Guidelines with their child. The student must also sign the same document and return it to the school before he or she can obtain computer privileges.

Media specialists and classroom teachers discuss the school's computer use policy with students. Students are required to pass a 15-point, true/false Computer Usage Test. They must score 100 percent to gain computer privileges. The test covers the district's Internet Guidelines and appropriate computer use. We issue a User Permit to a student only after he or she has successfully completed the Computer Usage Test. The User's Permit is signed by a teacher, the school's Media Specialist, and the student. Students must display the User's Permit at all times when using school computers.

Personal Responsibility

I am firmly against "blocking" software and "net nanny" mechanisms—for several reasons.

First, there's the cost. Any money spent on these programs is money you won't have for computer hardware and software. Second, even though many of the new censoring programs are very sophisticated, old or "cheap" programs usually don't think. They just block out words. Third, these blocking programs give parents and teachers alike a false sense of security: Hackers can break through the system of some of the older or cheaper programs. Finally, and this is my

I am firmly against "blocking" software and "net nanny" mechanisms.

strongest reason for opposing these mechanisms, I want to put my confidence in personal responsibility, not in a mechanical policing device.

In the long run, our students will be best served if we help them develop the good sense—and the good strong sense of responsibility—they will need to make sensible decisions and intelligent choices throughout their lives. We do them no favor if we set up a system that offers them no opportunity to practice personal responsibility.

Our students know they have to take responsibility for not abusing the system. If they don't follow the rules, they'll lose their computer privileges. The first year, we took our first student off within three hours of giving him his E-mail address. Because we've made the rules plain and made them tough, we've seen a decrease in abuse over the years. That first year, we had 11 students off computers for the whole year. This year, we had only one.

We do put a block on chatlines. Our school also has a system that allows us to see where everyone is on the computers. Students are not constantly monitored, but we check on them when we have reason to be concerned. In a way, this check-up is like a locker search that is conducted if we have probable cause.

Our students want the privilege of using technology. And they know there will be penalties if they abuse the privilege. This is not a complex system. And it's not perfect. But I know of none that is better.

Future Plans

One of my future goals is for my students to create more Web sites like the Dakota Conflict site. An important part of what my students have learned is that technology offers them a way to serve their community. The lesson I've learned is that I need to rely more on the talents of my students.

Students Are Technology Resources

My students are a wonderful technology resource. During the construction of the Dakota Conflict Web site, I discovered that one of my students had really mastered the program, MacPaint. So I had him teach the teams who thought they could use the MacPaint graphics program on their section of the Web site. I saw first-hand how effectively a knowledgeable student can teach the rest of the class.

Down the road, I plan to utilize the savvy kids in my class who excel in special areas. Some of them like Web Painter. Some of them know great sites for graphics. Others know Java Script, Avid Camera, and Adobe programs. And others have learned just by spending hours in front of the computer and poking around. These kids never read directions. They just get into a program and figure it out!

Gender Balance

I also intend to remain vigilant about avoiding gender bias and ensuring gender balance in technology. It would be tragic if technology came to be thought of as a "guy thing." Our society has enough stereotypes. We need to take care not to create more.

When I assign teams to be responsible for various parts of a Web site, I make sure that at least half of the team leaders are girls. And I like the fact that both media specialists I work with are female. When we're together, teaching the tricks of the tech trade, students see three females demonstrating their technological expertise. I think that sight delivers a valuable message—to young men as much as to young women.

Technology and the Mission of Public Schools

I believe that by integrating technology throughout a public school curriculum, Dakota Meadows Middle School has delivered powerful a message. We've made it our mission to ensure that Dakota Meadows graduates, whatever their parents' income level, will be as proficient with computers and as comfortable on the Internet as the graduates of private schools and the children of affluence. By making sure our students are at home in the information society and prepared for participation in a high-tech global village, we are advancing a primary goal of public education and making good on a precious promise of our democracy— equality of opportunity.

District Guidelines for Student Use of Internet Accounts

All Internet users are expected to abide by the generally accepted rules of computer and network etiquette. The following guidelines are the minimum taught to all district students:

1. Be polite. Do not get abusive in E-mail messages to others. School rules regarding harassment apply to electronic communication.

2. Use appropriate language. Do not swear, use vulgarities, or any other inappropriate language.

3. Do not reveal your personal address or the phone numbers of students or colleagues to unknown Internet users.

4. Be aware that E-mail is not guaranteed to be private. People who operate the system do have access to mail if there is probable cause to see it. Messages relating to or in support of illegal activities will be reported to the authorities.

5. There are some unacceptable uses of the networks. These include, but are not limited to:

   - Using the network for any illegal activity, including violation of copyright or other laws.
   - Using the network in ways that violate school policies and behavior standards.
   - Using the network for financial or commercial gain.
   - Degrading or disrupting equipment or system performance.
   - Invading the privacy of other individuals by accessing and/or vandalizing their computerized data.
   - Wasting technology resources, including bandwidth, file space, and printers.
   - Gaining unauthorized access to resources or entities.
   - Using an account owned by another user, with or without his/her permission.
   - Posting personal communications without the author's consent.

6. Any items produced by the students will not be posted to the Internet without their permission. If permission is granted, items will be considered fair use and available to the public.

Insights: _____

_____

_____

_____

_____

_____

Actions for Our School, District, or Association To Consider: _____

_____

_____

_____

_____

_____

_____

RADIO WAVES AND VIDEO CLIPS

A student-run company is the pinnacle of this class in radio and television production.

6 On a late fall afternoon, the producer and client are deep in discussion in the production company's conference room. They're looking over the shooting schedule for the project, a public service video on landlord-tenant laws that will be shown in law offices and libraries throughout the region. Shooting will begin in a few days on location, as well as on a set already being constructed a short distance from the conference room. The script has been approved, and the post production teams have been assigned. All that's left is to make sure the talent is available at a time convenient to both producer and client.

Although this may be an everyday scene in the world of advertising and video production, the company that has landed the job is not the usual advertising contractor. In fact, the producer sitting at the conference table with the attorney-client is my student, as are the members of the teams that will be working the cameras, completing the set in a nearby storage room, editing the videotape, and keying in the graphic elements in post production. These students aren't role-playing or merely completing a class assignment. They're performing a real job for a real community organization, preparing themselves for the real world of work.

STEPHEN D. LALONDE
University High School
Spokane, Washington

Learning for the Real World

In 1986 I returned to teaching after nine years in business and industry. Those interim years had given me a sense of how schools might prepare students more effectively for the real

I wanted to help students develop a better understanding of workplace attitudes, skills, and knowledge.

world by giving them a better understanding of workplace attitudes, skills, and knowledge, and an opportunity to develop those attributes even before they entered the workplace. I had first-hand knowledge of the need for a "school-to-work" transition program even before the term was in common use, and I had some ideas about how to meet that need. For the average teenager, a "real-world" education required a practical interface with the world of work while he or she was still in school. Since I had some experience with broadcast technology, I decided it was the hook I wanted to use to get students interested and involved in preparing for the workplace and their adult lives.

I submitted a proposal to the administration at University High School in Spokane, Washington, stating that I wished to introduce a class in radio and television (RTV) production that would help students develop a sense of responsibility and enable them to establish and practice interpersonal skills, group problem solving, teamwork, and time management. The proposal was accepted with one significant condition: the class would not add any costs to the school budget. Nearly a decade and a half later, RTV is one of the star programs of the school and the district.

I am a member of the English Department, as well as the Curriculum Coordinator for the Creative and Applied Arts Department at University High School. I divide my workweek between teaching classes in classical mythology and overseeing the RTV program. The mythology classes occupy about two-thirds of my time, and RTV the remainder. My school is one of two high schools in the Central Valley School District, a predominantly conservative white middle-class community with small but increasing enclaves of Mung and Russian immigrants. The student body reflects the demographics of the community.

The RTV Program

By the end of the 1990's, the RTV program had evolved from the initial elective introductory course—a basic hands-on class in which I taught students technical procedures and developed their writing skills in various scripting and advertising assignments. RTV was now a series of classes that moved from introductory material to higher levels of technical, administrative, and interpersonal skills. The original introductory course is now a prerequisite for advanced classes that students may enter only with the approval of the instructor.

Removing an Obstacle To Learning—Myself

Over the years, I've learned to get out of the way in order to let my students learn by teaching themselves and each other. In the early years of the program, I felt I had to know the operation of each piece of equipment in order to teach it, but as more and more equipment came in, I found myself frantically trying to keep up. About five years ago, I

finally decided to get out of the way and let the students do their own learning, and the program has quantum-leaped as a result. So the first thing I do when we get a new piece of equipment is make 10 photocopies of the manual and turn the students loose. They learn the machines—from the manuals and from each other, individually and in small groups.

Improved proficiency in reading is one outcome of this approach. In order to become adept at using the equipment that will enable them to produce videos, students must develop their technical reading skills. (One look at some of the equipment manuals should convince the most adamant doubter that these students have to become capable readers in order to function in the program.)

Whether students are classified as Advanced Placement, Individual Education Plan (IEP), or

any category of the spectrum in-between, they seem to experience equal degrees of success in the program. In fact, some of the tactile-kinesthetic students become the most capable equipment operators, no matter how sophisticated the equipment is.

Curriculum Progression and Structure

The RTV program is built on a very specific curriculum requiring a lot of hands-on activity and numerous assigned projects. Beginners learn the basics of equipment terminology and use,

I've learned to get out of the way in order to let my students learn by teaching each other.

as well as how to fill technical and talent positions in video production. We usually have 32

What an RTV Program Can Teach...

- Interpersonal skills
- Group problem-solving
- Teamwork
- Time management
- A sense of responsibility

And last, but not least,

- Ethics

students in the class, but since that is too large a group for a single media teacher to oversee effectively, advanced students help beginners throughout the program. One of our mottoes is "If you know it, you must teach it."

Advanced courses are increasingly student-centered until we reach the program's pinnacle called Viable Vision Video Production. Viable Vision is a student-run company that produces commercial-quality video for businesses and organizations throughout the Pacific Northwest. The company's Board of Directors, which meets regularly to make policy and project decisions, is composed of students elected by their peers.

Intro to Radio and Television Production

Learning the Jobs

The initial course begins with a project that rotates each student through several technician positions behind the camera and one talent position in front of the camera. Typically, the project includes a student in the talent spot at a podium delivering a tongue-twister article in his or her best newscaster persona while other students operate the cameras and the tape deck, and snap the marker-board—the hand-held board with the hinged top used on a movie or video set to identify the scene and "take." I direct this first project, and it's the only time in the entire course that I perform a talent or technician role. Advanced students quickly introduce beginning students to each piece of equipment.

Electrical Safety and Radio/TV History

Next we have a short unit on electrical safety, which includes a section on electrical terms and formulas, followed by a brief and simplified history of radio and television. These units move quickly. They are not difficult, and there are many support materials readily available.

Radio Projects

Radio projects follow, culminating with each student writing and recording a commercial, a public service announcement, and a news spot. This unit includes instruction in copywriting, enunciation and pronunciation, timing, and the technical aspects of recording and editing audio. Practical demonstrations and many samples, both professional and student, are provided. At the end of the unit, each student turns in a tape with the three recorded projects, the scripts, and a photocopy of the news article from which he or she has paraphrased the news spot. In this cluster of activities, writing skills are practiced over and over and honed to a professional finish.

The Practical Exam

The Practical Exam is the next unit. Students spend several days receiving detailed instruction on each of the basic pieces of equipment they will operate in the television production projects. These include cameras, tape decks, video special-effects generators, the audio mixer board, microphones, and cables and connectors. I allow several more days for the students to work together or individually, practicing the various elements of video production.

The exam itself takes several days because we require each student to rotate through stations to demonstrate each skill and operate all the switches, knobs, and dials, as well as to name all the cables, connectors, and equipment components. Advanced students and I do the testing at the various stations, often assisted by graduates who return for this significant rite of passage.

Television Commercials

The Practical Exam leads to preparation for television commercials. Students view sample commercials (as if contemporary teens need to see any more ads) and storyboards, which show the video and audio components in a format similar to comic strips. Then the students themselves prepare storyboards for an original television commercial. After grading the storyboards, I choose five for the class to produce. The students are then divided into five production groups, each of which is led by the writer of one of the chosen storyboards. These production groups, which involve each student in the class in a technical or talent position, give excellent practice in teamwork and group problem solving.

News, Weather, and Sports

During the final weeks of the class, students develop and tape a "broadcast." The class is divided evenly into three groups (news, weather, and sports) and spends two days researching articles and weather information. Students build the set. Over the next two or three days, they complete the blocking. Dozens of

Video production groups give excellent practice in teamwork and joint problem solving.

takes are done on each portion of the project. Before the final day of class, the advanced students edit the television commercials and news-weather-sports projects into a single program. On the last day, the students watch their program and a program from a past class and then do a written comparative critique for the final exam.

Advanced RTV

In the advanced class, students begin learning and refining post-

My challenge was how to get equipment for the class without spending school funds.

production skills, such as video editing. This requires not only selecting and organizing the footage to be used in a show, but also combining text and graphic elements with the footage, achieving audio consistency, and

performing other tasks that create the final video. Each student starts to build a portfolio that will include all the work done in the introductory course, as well as in subsequent classes.

At any point after successful completion of the introductory class, a student may submit a completed application form to join Viable Vision Video Production. The Viable Vision Board of Directors exercises responsibility and interpersonal skills by reviewing the applications, conducting interviews, and selecting the students to join the company. The activities of Viable Vision overlap with the advanced course in the last trimester of the year.

At the end of senior year, each student must produce a complete portfolio. This will include video tape, audio tape, and all project paperwork, plus a resume, letters of recommendation from satisfied clients,

certification documents based on a technical and talent certification process, a list of all projects on which he or she has worked, and commendations from clients and school officials.

Building the Technology Base

Getting Affordable Equipment

In 1986, my initial challenge was how to assemble the technological elements for a Radio and Television class without spending any school funds. The first place I looked was in the district warehouse where obsolete equipment was stored.

My search produced black and white cameras, some old reel-to-reel video tape-recorders, and some audio-cassette recorders. I brought an old Beta VCR from home as well as some microphones and an audio amplifier left over from my "rock and roll" days. As my first out-of-pocket expenditure (but certainly not the last), I purchased ten regular clamp-on type work lights from a local hardware store, and we were in business. We didn't add anything else in the first year.

I made a list of items that would enhance the program and noted what I was willing to pay for each one. Then I began making a regular activity of going to yard sales and auctions, looking for anything that might add to the equipment for the class. I often found audio-cassette recorders, microphones, VCR's, and televisions. Sometimes when I mentioned what I was doing, people would donate items, especially at yard sales within the service area of University High School.

I requested a one-day substitute from my principal so I could have the time to go to local radio and television stations to encourage them to donate old equipment as they upgraded their studios. My initial visits to broadcasters resulted in several significant donations, a success we've repeated on subsequent occasions.

Several years into the program, the district administration allowed me to make several purchases that moved us out of black and white into color video production. We also were able to acquire two editing tape decks and an edit controller, two studio cameras, and some monitors. Part of the impetus for this was our need to rent color cameras to tape some of the commercial projects we had begun to undertake.

Additionally, the parent booster club that raises money for special projects contributed substantially, purchasing high-quality microphones, hard cases for transporting equipment to on-site shoots, and special effects equipment.

One day, while talking with a friend who works as a technician at a local hospital, I discovered that the hospital had a very sophisticated video production facility. My friend arranged for me to talk to the hospital administrator about our video program. Since then, the hospital has become one of our most generous contributors of equipment, which, even though it is being replaced by newer technology, is perfectly usable for us.

When one local machine company decided to close its training

My initial visits to radio and TV broadcasters resulted in several significant donations.

video division in 1997, it donated to our program all the studio and field equipment, including cameras, tripods, monitors, and other vital items.

Computers

One of the most important elements of quality video production is careful editing, which—along with other post-production tasks—requires sturdy and reliable computers. Our Mac Power PC 6100/60AV is the real workhorse. The Mac enables us to do editing and output to videotape, digital audio acquisition and editing, digital photo acquisition, and small-frame

A local machine company donated cameras, tripods, monitors, and other vital items.

digital video editing. We also use it for animation, test-taking with auto scoring, and a host of other applications. In addition, we have a couple of Mac Pluses for word processing and test preparation. Other tools in our equipment armory include a Broadcast Titler, which is used for some of our graphics work, the Disney Animation Studio, which allows for full-frame animation projects, and the Toaster 4000, with which we generate all kinds of video special effects.

Viable Vision Video Production—from Simple to Sophisticated

Since the mid-1990's, we have been producing video projects for businesses and organizations within the larger community, and word has gotten around about the quality of work our students do. Viable Vision productions range from simple event coverage for University High School to sophisticated public service announcements (PSA's) for organizations throughout the Pacific Northwest.

One of the simplest and shortest projects is our annual video of the Lilac Princess Coronation at Spokane's Lilac Festival. Each high school in the Spokane area holds a pageant to select its princess, and a queen is then selected from among the princesses. For several years we have taped the pageant at our school with full production—that is, as though it were a live event on television, including graphics screens, text overlays, multi-camera angles with special effects, and scrolling credits. We set up six tape decks so that at the end of the evening each one of the five contestants gets her own full production copy, and we have our master tape for the archive.

Promotional Videos

Our out-of-classroom success really began four years into the RTV program with a public service announcement against drinking and driving. It ran on one of the local television stations for ten weeks during the prom season. That project was followed by a product promotional video for a music store that we shot on location in a nearby hotel. This production led in turn to a corporate promotional video for that hotel chain. Since then, we have completed dozens of major projects for businesses and organizations outside the school, in addition to projects for the school.

News 101

As the community learned of our activities, we were asked to participate in a program called News 101, in which students prepared teen-related news stories that aired on a local station's evening news. Of 17 articles the students produced, 16 were aired, four were nominated for a national newsreel, and two were chosen for inclusion in the newsreel. One student—Josh Streufert, the first president of Viable Vision—received a News 101 scholarship to the film school at Evergreen State College.

A Public Service

Although our productions are created free of charge as a public service, the compensation we receive is substantial in the education every project provides to each student. We are also "compensated" by the letters of praise clients send when productions are completed. Clients often make cash donations to the program, provide in-kind support, or lend us props and costumes. The Viable Vision students use their growing interpersonal skills to negotiate for loan items. They demonstrate their responsibility by seeing that borrowed materials are returned in good order as soon as they are no longer needed.

The Northwest Justice Project

One of the most complex learning experiences the students have had was the 1997 production of a video on Washington state's landlord-tenant laws.

When the Northwest Justice Project contacted me at the beginning of the year about the possibility of doing such a legal issues program, I gave the information to the Viable Vision Chairperson. He then called a meeting of the Board members.

Our success began with a public service announcement against drinking and driving.

The Board members called a meeting with the prospective clients and made "the pitch," showing several samples of past projects and telling about Viable Vision programs and procedures. The students received an immediate go-ahead from the client, demonstrating that they could put into practice valuable lessons about the delicate business of closing a sale.

If You Want to Establish a Real-World RTV Program...

- Begin with an emphasis on process and then set increasingly high standards for product.
- Bring your principal on board to open doors in the community.
- Develop a relationship with your local radio and television stations.
- Arrange with your school district to facilitate used equipment purchases from private individuals, yard sales, auctions, etc.
- Find the independent video and audio producers in your community who might provide their old equipment when they upgrade.
- Locate an electronics technician willing to help with—and teach students about—maintenance and repair.
- Attend seminars and workshops on videography and filmmaking given by universities and equipment vendors.
- Find a reliable vendor who will help you design and acquire new equipment and supplies.
- Be careful not to take work away from the people who help you.

The students spent the following week working on production ideas and storyboarding a possible visual sequence for the program. At the next meeting, the client was pleased with the presentation and approved it. Although we usually begin working on the script at that point, the Northwest Justice Project had a professional scriptwriter already committed to it. We waited until we received the script before a student was chosen to be the producer. She arranged for another meeting with the client to go over a shooting schedule.

This project was the first in which the students were directing adult professional actors—another step in refining their interpersonal skills. Much of the video was shot over a two-day period on location in an apartment complex. Working in shifts during this part of the production, students had an opportunity to take responsibility for their activities and practice time management.

The rest of the video was shot at University High School, where we converted a storage room off the library into a lawyer's office. One of the teachers at University, a practicing lawyer who decided he wanted to teach and coach, was recruited to be the narrator. We hung his credentials on the wall, and shooting began after school and during his prep period. After all the raw video was shot, he came in during class to do the voice-overs.

While the shooting was going on, the producer had a group of students preparing the graphic elements that would be keyed over the video. (Keying-in is placing text and graphics over the picture.) They also prepared solid screens of bulleted lists and text with no video background.

The Aesthetics of "Toasting"

Although my generation thought color film was a vast artistic improvement on black and white footage, my students consider custom-made antique segments a desirable aesthetic element in their productions. So in post-production, one editing crew took the location video and "toasted" it. The crew treated it like an old-time silent movie with black and white action shots interspersed with text screens. The black and white sequence depicted an individual looking for an apartment and reaching an agreement with a landlord. In order to be toasted, the color video had to be run

through one processor to strip out the color, another to add "scratches and dust", and a third to add the text screens. Finally, the students digitally modified some honky-tonk piano music to provide the audio track. Such complex post-production activities tend to be labor-intensive, and by their very nature involve massive group problem-solving.

Segments of the same location footage in color, without scratches and dust, and with the general background music of the rest of the tape, were used to demonstrate the legal issues discussed in the rest of the video.

The finished project ran 27 minutes and was completed two weeks into the summer vacation. The seniors who had committed to the project continued to work on it until it was completed, even though they had graduated three weeks earlier. The attorney who represented the client was so pleased that she wrote to

Viable Vision. She not only thanked the students for a high-quality production that spoke clearly to its audience, but also indicated that the Northwest Justice Project would like to

The complex post-production activities involve massive group problem solving.

build a library of such informational videos produced by Viable Vision.

The Next Step

The next big step for the video production program at University High School is to move into digital video editing. All of our project editing now uses analog equipment. Digital editing will probably increase our output by four or five times because of the speed and non-linear aspect of the process.

Farther down the road, I would like to see us have a van outfitted for remote (on location) shooting, complete with editing equipment. After all, we didn't get this far without ambitious goals!

Preparing for the Real World

When the doctor told me in the early months of 1999 that the cold I hadn't been able to shake had turned into pneumonia and

The last thing I did before collapsing was send my students a new project by E-mail.

that I must stay home if I wanted to recover, my first thought was of my RTV students. I wanted to ensure that they would be able to continue the steady progress they'd been making during the fall and early winter.

The last thing I did before collapsing was send my students a new project by E-mail. They were to develop a media campaign for a delicious new candy. They had to name it; plan and produce TV, radio, and print advertising for it; and design its packaging. In other words, they were to model an intricate professional real-world activity that would require all the teamwork, time management, and interpersonal skills they had been developing over the past months.

In the real world, enormous budgets drive—and huge revenues ride on—such activities. Although I would guide my students and answer their questions via E-mail from my distant sickbed, they would do all the creative and technical work themselves. It was up to them to shoulder the responsibility of finishing it on deadline—by the time I got back to school.

My students came through with flying colors. They came up with a name—Ambrosia, scripted and produced advertising spots, wrote copy for space and radio advertising, designed an attractive package, and became so involved in the project that they began to work on creating the candy itself! I was the cheerleader. They were the professionals doing a real-world job themselves, learning for their future lives.

Video Production Portfolio Checklist

Name_____ Date_____

Your semester grade is determined largely by the portfolio you will be building that documents the work you've done this semester. You should include the following items in your portfolio:

☐ Journal (the daily written record of in-class activities).

☐ Time log (the record of time spent outside of class on any activity related to audio and video production).

☐ Audio tape (or tapes) with samples of all video projects you created or to which you contributed.

☐ Video tape (or tapes) with samples of all video projects you created or to which you contributed.

☐ Copies of any "thank you's" or certificates of recognition you received for work that you did as part of this class.

☐ Copies of all promotional materials you created (e.g., posters for a radio program or announcements of a New 101 airing).

☐ List of projects you worked on (in or out of class) and the role(s) you played.

Written explanation (below) of any other information you feel should be considered in your grade. (Attach additional sheets if necessary.)

Reader Reflections

Insights: _____

_____

_____

_____

_____

Actions for Our School, District, or Association To Consider: _____

_____

_____

_____

_____

_____

Selected Resources

Books

Barron, Ann E. and Gary W. Orwig. 1997. *New Technologies for Education: A Beginner's Guide.* Libraries Unlimited, Inc.

Breivik, P.S. and J.A. Senn. 1998. *Information Literacy.* Washington D.C.: National Education Association.

Brunner, Cornelia and William Talley. 1999. *The Media Literacy Handbook: An Educator's Guide to Bringing New Media into the Classroom.* Doubleday & Company, Inc.

Cummins, Jim and Dennis Sayers. 1997. *Brave New Schools: Challenging Cultural Illiteracy Through Global Learning Networks.* St. Martin's Press.

Forcier, Richard C. 1998. *The Computer as an Educational Tool: Productivity and Problem Solving.* Prentice Hall.

Healy, Jane M. 1998. *Failure to Connect: How Computers Affect Our Children's Minds—for Better and Worse.* Simon & Schuster Trade.

Heinich, Robert, James D. Russell, Michael Molenda and Sharon E. Smaldino. 1998. *Instructional Media and Technologies for Learning.* Prentice Hall.

Jonassen, David H., Kyle L. Peck and Brent G. Wilson. 1998. *Learning with Technology: A Constructivist Perspective.* Prentice Hall.

Kent, Todd W. and Robert F. McNergney. 1998. *Will Technology Really Change Education?: From Blackboard to Web.* Corwin Press, Inc.

McCormack, Colin and David Jones. 1997. *Building a Web-Based Education System.* Wiley, John & Sons, Inc.

Ryder, Randall James and Tom Hughes. 1997. *Internet for Educators 2nd ED.* Prentice Hall.

Schrum, Lynne and Berenfeld. 1997. *Teaching and Learning in the Information Age: A Guide to Educational Telecommunications.* Allyn & Bacon.

Technology for Diverse Learners. 1997. Washington, D.C.: National Education Association.

Williams, Bard. 1997. *Internet for Teachers, with CD-ROM.* IDG Books Worldwide.

Magazines

Classroom Connect. Classroom Connect, Inc., 431 Madrid Avenue, Torrance, CA 90501-1430.

DV (Digital Video) Magazine. Imas Publishing Co., 411 Borel Ave., Suite 100, San Mateo, CA 94402.

Multimedia Schools. Information Today, Inc., 143 Old Marlton Pike, Medford, NJ 08055-8750.

School Library Media Activities Monthly. LMS Associated L.L.C., 17 E. Henrietta St., Baltimore, MD 21230-3010.

TV Technology Magazine. Miller Freeman Publishing Co., P.O. Box 1214, Falls Church, VA 22041-9808.

Videos
Computers From the Inside Out. VHS, 1996. Tapeworm.

Plugging Into Technology. VHS, 1996. Washington, D.C.: National Education Association.

Technology: Hype or Hope. VHS, 1997. Washington, D.C.: National Education Association.

Technologies of the Gods. 1998; VHS, 60 min. Mystic Fire.

Web Sites
Information on integrating curriculum and multimedia can be located at http://www.edu.gov.mb.ca/metks4/tech/currtech/cmi/integrate.html

Looking for technology and Internet integration resources? Click on to http://www.union.k12.ia.us/ukhs/Educational/integ_tech.htm.

For a chance to see how teachers are using technology in their classrooms visit the following sites: http://www.siec.k12.in.us/%7Ewest/slides/integrate/sld001.htm, http://www.richmond.edu/is/faculty/techlinks.html, http://www.21ct.org,

http://epiphany.simplenet.com/mccarthy/lessons/index.html, http://www.videonics.com, or http://www.audio-technica.com/index2.html.

To learn about writing, editing, and Web site design and development, check out http://www.marketek.com

Digital video resources can be found at http://www.dv.com.

A resource for online professional development courses that focus on technology can be found at http://www.att.com/learningnetwork/virtualacademy.

If you are a teacher of grades K-6, look up www.Creativeclassroom.org/.

http://www.electronic-school.com is the school technology authority.

Kids can connect with classrooms from 100 countries with http://www.epals.com/

Register your school's home page with International School Web Site Registry. http://web66.coed.umn.edu/schools.html.

Software, CDs, or Multimedia
101 Dalmatians, Disney Interactive/Win/Mac/CD.

Animal Behavior is a compendium of words, images, and sounds about animals by Optical Data Corporation. http://www.opticaldata.com.

Notes:

_____

_____

_____

_____

_____

_____

Blaster Learning System: 3R's for Ages 6-9, Cendant/Knowledge Adventure/Win3.1/95/Mac/CD

Classroom Publisher is a tool for teachers to create seating charts, newsletters, banners, and other materials. Staz Software, http://stazware.com/cpub.html.

ClarisWorks (now sold as AppleWorks and as ClarisWorks for Kids) is an integrated word processing, spreadsheet, database, and drawing program. Apple computer, http://www.apple.com.

Creative Writer 2.0, Microsoft Corporation/Win3.1/95/CD.

Earth Quest, DK Multimedia/Win/Mac/CD.

Fun 4 Kids: Hellos Kitty, Baby Felix, and Friends, Fox Interactive/Win 3.1/95/98/Mac/CD.

Grossology, SegaSoft/Win95/Mac/CD

Highlights at WWW. Teachernet.com/html/cds.DNA lists kid's favorite CD-ROMs.

HyperStudio is a multimedia authoring tool that combines words, images, and sound to create electronic "cards." Roger Wagner Publishing, http://www.hyperstudio.com.

Microsoft Exchange is an e-mail program that often comes bundled with other Microsoft products. Microsoft, http://www.microsoft.com.

My First Amazing History Explorer, DK Multimedia/Win/Mac/CD.

Success Builder Math Library, The Learning Company/Win/Mac/CD.

Writing Tutor, Simon & Schuster Interactive/Win3.1/95/CD.

Organizations
Association for Educational Communications and Technology, 1025 Vermont Ave., N.W., Suite 820, Washington, D.C. 20005.

Center for Educational Leadership and Technology, 165 Forest St., Marlborough, MA 01752.

Center for Leadership in School Reform, 950 Breckenridge Lane, Suite 200, Louisville, KY 40207.

Computer Learning Foundation, P.O. Box 60007, Palo Alto, CA 94306-0007.

International Technology Education Association, 1914 Association Drive, Reston, Va. 22091-1502.

Media Workshops Foundation, 9911 Paramount Boulevard, Suite 261, Downey, CA 90240.

The National Center for the Study of Writing and Literacy, 5513 Tolman Hall, University of California, Berkeley, CA 94704-1670.

Technology and Information Educational Services, 1925 West Country Rd., B, Roseville, MN 55113-2791.

Notes:
_____
_____
_____
_____
_____
_____

Personal Resources

Individuals: _____

_____

_____

_____

Organizations: _____

_____

_____

_____

Publications: _____

_____

_____

_____

Glossary

Analog
Electronic transmission accomplished by adding signals of varying frequency or amplitude to carrier waves of a given frequency of alternating electro-magnetic current. Analog is usually represented as a series of sine waves. Broadcast and phone transmissions have conventionally used analog technology.

CD-ROM
A compact disc that can hold a large amount of soft-ware. ROM stands for read-only memory, which means you can access the software on a CD-ROM, but cannot alter it or write over it.

Chat (Synchronous)
Two or more people sharing a text-based conversa-tion, like a conference call, where everyone needs to be online at the same time.

Cyberspace
The electronic space created when many computers are connected together.

Database
A collection of data that is organized so that its con-tents can easily be accessed, managed, and updated.

Digital
Electronic technology that generates, stores, and processes data in terms of two states: positive (1) and non-positive (0). Thus, data transmitted or stored with digital technology is expressed as a string of 0's and 1's. It is primarily used with new physical communications media.

E-mail (Electronic Mail)
A means of sending information electronically, via computer, from one person to another, or from one to many. Sometimes called asynchronous communication.

Ethernet
A fast and cheap networking design that has become a popular way to exchange information between computers on a network. Ethernet allows both files and peripherals to be shared.

Firewall
A firewall is a set of related programs, located at a network gateway server, that protects the resources of a private network from users from other networks. Basically, a firewall, working closely with a router program, filters all network packets to determine whether to forward them toward their destination.

Hardware
Computer-related components, such as the CPU, disk drives, monitor, and printer.

Hit
A hit is a single file request in the log of a Web serv-er. A request for an HTML page with three graphic images will result in four hits in the log: one for the HTML file and one for each of the graphic image files. While a hit is a meaningful measure of how much traffic a server handles, it can be a misleading indicator of how many pages are being looked at.

Hypertext Markup Language (HTML)

A set of "markup" codes inserted in a file intended for display on a World Wide Web browser. The markup tells the Web browser how to display a web page's words and images for the user.

HyperCard

Software for Macintosh computers that provides an easy method of creating hypertext presentations.

Import

To move an item or file into an application or environment which is different than that native to it.

Internet

The worldwide network of computers, switches and routers that is collaboratively maintained and upgraded by users, service providers and telecommunications companies. It began in the early 1970s as a U.S. Defense Department network built to share data with several research universities and defense contractors. Later altered, added to and privatized, it grew as more and more businesses and universities created gateways to it. Today, the Internet has over 200 million computers connected to it.

Laptop Computer

A portable computer that has a flat screen and usually weighs less than a dozen pounds. It uses AC power and/or batteries.

LaserDisc

A technology and the physical medium used in storing and providing programmed access to a large database of text, pictures, and other objects, including motion video and full multimedia presentation.

Link

The URL, or web address, embedded in another document, so that if you click on the highlighted text or button referring to the link, you retrieve the outside URL.

Local Area Network (LAN)

A LAN is a network of interconnected workstations sharing the resources of a single processor or server within a relatively small geographic area. A local area network may serve as few as four or five users or may serve several thousand. Typically, a suite of application programs can be kept on the LAN server.

Macintosh

Computer developed by Apple Computer Inc. The Macintosh was one of the first computers to use a graphical user interface. Today, Apple continues to produce many different models of Macintosh, which are used mainly for desktop publishing and multimedia production.

Mailing List

An E-mail-based discussion list. People "subscribe," and from then on, any E-mail sent to the list is received by all subscribers.

Mouse

A mouse is a small device that a computer user pushes across a desk surface in order to point to a

Notes:

_____

_____

_____

_____

_____

_____

place on a display screen and to select one or more actions to take from that position.

Modem

A modem modulates outgoing digital signals from a computer or other digital device to analog signals for a conventional copper twisted-pair telephone line and demodulates the incoming analog signal and converts it to a digital signal for the digital device.

Multimedia

A document composed of multiple forms of communication, such as text, audio, and/or video.

Network

In information technology, a network is a series of points or nodes interconnected by communication paths. Networks can interconnect with other networks and contain sub-networks. Networks can also be characterized in terms of spatial distance as local area networks (LANs), metropolitan area networks (MANs), and wide area networks (WANs).

Personal Computer (PC)

In its more general usage, a PC (personal computer) is a computer designed for use by one person at a time. The term "PC" is also commonly used to describe an "IBM-compatible" personal computer in contradistinction to an Apple Macintosh computer. The distinction is both technical and cultural.

Pixel

The display on a monitor is made up of a collection of dots called pixels. For monochrome screens, a pixel contains one dot. For color displays, a pixel contains three dots (red, green, and blue). By varying the intensity of the dots, you can display up to 256 shades of gray or millions of colors. Pixel stands for picture element.

RAM (Random Access Memory)

RAM is the place in a computer where the operating system, application programs, and data in current use are kept so they can be quickly reached by the computer's processor. RAM is much faster to read from and write to than the other kinds of storage in a computer—the hard disk, floppy disk, and CD-ROM. However, the data in RAM stays there only as long as your computer is running. When you turn the computer off, RAM loses its data.

Scanner

A device that interprets a photograph or printed document and converts it into pixels for display on a computer.

Server

In general, a server is a computer program that provides services to other computer programs in the same or other computers. The computer that a server program runs in is also frequently referred to as a server (though it may contain a number of server and client programs). In the client/server programming model, a server is a program that awaits and fulfills requests from client programs in the same or other computers.

Notes:

_____

_____

_____

_____

_____

_____

Snail Mail
A disparaging term for paper-based mail.

Software
Software is a general term for the various kinds of programs used to operate computers and related devices. Software can be thought of as the variable part of a computer and hardware the invariable part. Software is often divided into application software (programs that do work users are directly interested in) and system software (which includes operating systems and any program that supports application software). It is usually packaged on CD-ROM and diskettes. Today, much purchased software is downloaded over the Internet.

Spreadsheet
Software that simulates a paper spreadsheet, or worksheet, in which columns of numbers are summed for budgets and plans.

URL (Uniform Resource Locator)
The address of a file (resource) accessible on the Internet. The URL contains the name of the protocol required to access the resource, a domain name that identifies a specific computer on the Internet, and a hierarchical description of a file location on the computer. On the Web (which uses the Hypertext Transfer Protocol), an example of a URL is: http://www.ci.kingston.ny.us/. An HTTP URL can be for any Web page, not just a home page, or any individual file. For example, the following URL would bring you the whatis.com logo image: http://whatis.com/whatisAnim2.gif.

Video-conferencing
A video communications session among two or more people in separate locations.

Windows
A feature of an operating system (Microsoft or Apple OS, e.g.).

Word Processing
Software that provides you with tools necessary to edit and format text. Word processors commonly include a window for entering text, the ability to control the format of text (bold, italics, size), indenting, margins, the ability to check spelling, etc.

World Wide Web (WWW or Web)
A collection of Internet sites that offer text and graphics and sound and animation resources through the hypertext transfer protocol (http).

Zip Drive
A compact, high-capacity storage device that uses removable disks.

Notes:

_____

_____

_____

_____

_____

_____